BLUNTING THE SWORD:
Budget Policy and the Future of Defense

For sale by the U.S. Government Printing Office
Superintendent of Documents, Mail Stop: SSOP, Washington, DC 20402-9328
ISBN 0-16-045229-5

Blunting the Sword:
Budget Policy and the Future of Defense

Dennis S. Ippolito

1994
National Defense University
Washington, DC

National Defense University Press Publications

To increase general knowledge and inform discussion, the Institute for National Strategic Studies, through its publication arm the NDU Press, publishes McNair Papers; proceedings of University- and Institute-sponsored symposia; books relating to U.S. national security, especially to issues of joint, combined, or coalition warfare, peacekeeping operations, and national strategy; and a variety of briefer works designed to circulate contemporary comment and offer alternatives to current policy. The Press occasionally publishes out-of-print defense classics, historical works, and other especially timely or distinguished writing on national security.

NDU Press publications are sold by the U.S. Government Printing Office. For ordering information, call (202) 783-3238 or write to the Superintendent of Documents, U.S. Government Printing Office, Washington, DC 20402.

Library of Congress Cataloguing in Publication Data

Ippolito, Dennis S.
    Blunting the sword: budget policy and the future of defense / Dennis S. Ippolito
        p. cm
    Includes bibliographical references and index.
    1. United States—Armed Forces—Appropriations and expenditures—History.   2. United States. Dept of Defense—Appropriations and expenditures—History.   3. United States—Economic policy—1981–. 4. World politics—1989–. I. Title.
UA25.5.I67 1994
355.6'22'097309045—dc20   94–8106
                                                            CIP

For my family, *fide et amore sustinemur*

Contents

Tables

Figures

Foreword

Since the end of the Cold War, a number of unusual defense budgeting issues have cropped up—among them, the "sacred" programs, the myth of reduced forces, the illusion of budget windfalls, and the increased risk in decisions about force structure, readiness, and modernization. The issues tend to boil down to a choice between smaller forces or less modern forces. Professor Dennis Ippolito of Southern Methodist University examines this dilemma from the perspective of an analyst outside the Defense establishment, one with no personal agenda and no particular constituency.

At the root of the dilemma, Ippolito suggests, is the lack of a public perception of a "clear and immediate threat," such as that which unified national purpose during the Cold War. He argues that presidential commitment to and national consensus for a strong defense need to be restored. Otherwise, as he explains, U.S. defense will fall to levels grossly inadequate for a global superpower, exacting a heavy price in quality, readiness, and capabilities. He agrees with those who suggest that severe cutbacks in defense levels will have only a marginal impact on *national, structural* budget deficits, but cause serious damage to important and enduring military capabilities. Finally, using hard facts and financial data, he shows that the time for action is now because rebuilding a demolished defense structure a few years hence would be even more expensive, perhaps prohibitively so.

NDU is pleased to publish this illuminating and objective study of a major national defense problem during this period of great change and uncertainty.

PAUL G. CERJAN
Lieutenant General, U.S. Army
President, National Defense University

Acknowledgments

This book had its genesis in a lecture I was invited to present at the Army War College in 1990. Lieutenant General Paul G. Cerjan, at that time serving as Commandant of the Army War College, had heard me speak on federal budget policy and encouraged me to develop the theme of nondefense budget constraints for the faculty and students at the War College. The response to that lecture and to the several Commandant's Lectures I have subsequently been privileged to offer convinced me that a long-term analysis of the budgetary context within which defense spending needs are assessed would provide some immediate guidance to decisionmakers inside and outside the defense community. I hope this book fulfills that purpose.

I am indebted to General Cerjan and to Major General William A. Stofft, his successor as Commandant, for their encouragement of this project. I also appreciate the assistance of several current and former members of the War College faculty, including Colonel William A. Larson, Colonel Daniel W. Palmer, and Colonel Robert B. Tinsman, during my visits to Carlisle Barracks. The gracious treatment and distinctive professionalism I encountered made these visits a genuine pleasure.

At Southern Methodist University, Linda Cooke and Kim Essency have provided superb assistance in the research and preparation of the manuscript. Dr. Frederick T. Kiley, of the National Defense University Press, has been wonderfully helpful in bringing the project to completion.

The customary disclaimer that a book's errors and shortcomings are one's own applies with special force in this instance. The responsibility for this analysis and interpretation is, for better or worse, truly my own.

BLUNTING THE SWORD:
Budget Policy and the Future of Defense

1. Why Defense Budgets Are Unstable

AS THE UNITED STATES ENTERS the post-Cold War era, defense planners face a challenging confluence of political and budgetary pressures. Political pressures to accelerate defense budget reductions keep mounting, as "peace dividends" are claimed for various other programs. The Clinton administration's director of the Office of Management and Budget (OMB), Leon E. Panetta, once warned his former congressional colleagues that "We need some authoritative answers . . . [and] shouldn't make the defense budget just a grab bag for tax cuts or for spending. . . . A number of members have probably spent the so-called peace dividend 30 times over in various proposals."[1] Nevertheless, one of the Clinton administration's earliest policy initiatives was to double the defense budget cuts that candidate Bill Clinton had advocated during the 1992 presidential campaign.

The defense spending reductions now being implemented, however, are only part of the problem. Defense planners face even more severe long-term funding cutbacks because of nondefense budget policy constraints. Future growth in federal entitlements and other mandatory spending programs will significantly limit the resources available to support defense programs, and, with budget deficits certain to remain at high levels, defense programs will be caught in a tightening squeeze between domestic program needs and deficit-control efforts.

The United States is entering an era during which it will be especially difficult to balance strategic concerns and budgetary pressures. Past failures to maintain this balance have proved costly—extreme defense budget cutbacks after World War II and again after the Vietnam War so severely jeopardized U.S. military capabilities that sharp buildups in defense spending had to be implemented quickly. These buildups were facilitated by relatively flexible federal budgets that could accommodate

3

tradeoffs to defense. With discretionary spending margins continuing to shrink, because of entitlement program growth and large structural deficits, it will be much harder in the future to reverse defense cutbacks when and if the necessity arises.

All sides in the defense policy debate acknowledge that defense budgets will decline from their Cold War peaks. Significant force level reductions, major procurement cancellations, and real spending cutbacks were initiated by the Bush administration and are being expedited by the Clinton administration.[2] The central issue, then, is not whether defense budgets will be cut but rather what will be the scale and timing of the reductions, and the concern is that these decisions will be dictated by an increasingly constrained budget process that undercuts responsible military planning. Just how seriously future planning will be compromised is uncertain, but the history of past defense budget cycles is not reassuring. A clear understanding of these cycles and of their current budgetary relevance adds an indispensable historical perspective to the debate about how to balance strategy and budgets.[3]

Cycles of Defense Budgeting

Since the end of World War II, defense spending levels have been very volatile. Each of the conventional indicators— budget shares, gross national product (GNP) and gross domestic product (GDP) shares, and real outlays—has fluctuated widely.[4] Real spending for defense, for example, has been highly unstable, with several pronounced postwar cycles (figure 1).

The volatility in defense budget levels, particularly during peacetime, is largely unrelated to changes in external threats and in the national security environment. As Weidenbaum, and others, have emphasized, the oscillations "between aggressive calls for accelerated spending and periods of declining military budgets" demonstrate the "changing internal response to a relatively constant set of external factors."[5] An important consequence of this politically driven instability, concludes Weidenbaum, "is hasty planning of military force structures followed by cancellation or inefficient stretch-outs of expensive

4

FIGURE 1. *Defense outlays, fiscal years 1940-1990 (in billions of FY 1982 constant dollars)*

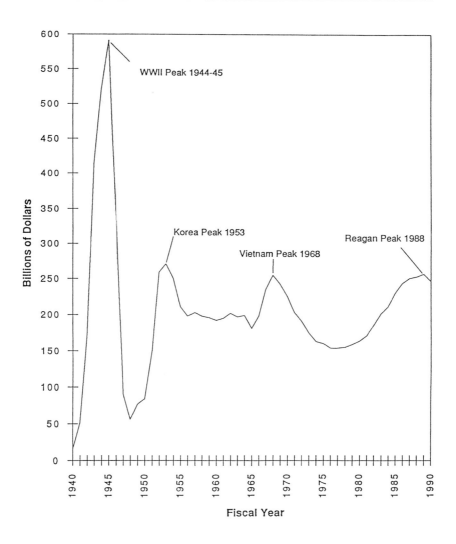

Source: Compiled by author

weapon systems, a waste of the vast resources devoted to national defense."[6]

The uncertainties in defense budgeting complicate strategic planning, since it is difficult to sustain coherent planning during either abrupt buildups or sharp cutbacks, especially when Congress intervenes frequently in policy decisions.[7] While defense planning would benefit from stable, predictable funding, the federal budget process is highly sensitive to countervailing forces, perhaps the most enduring of which is the pressure to shift defense funding to domestic programs with more immediate and tangible benefits. The budget process is also responsive to fiscal policy considerations, such as deficit reduction and spending control, that usually impose disproportionate constraints on defense.

During the 1950s, a strategic consensus and strong presidential leadership partially insulated defense from these countervailing forces, but the strategic and institutional supports necessary to sustain stable defense budgeting have eroded over the past few decades. As a result, it has become more and more difficult to protect long-term defense needs. The post-Cold War defense budgeting framework appears to be especially challenging, since it comprises all of the strategic, institutional, and budgetary vulnerabilities that place defense at special risk (table 1).

The persistent tension between defense and domestic spending needs has its programmatic roots in the New Deal.[8] The Roosevelt administration's legislative agenda encompassed the two broad categories of domestic programs against which defense has subsequently competed. First, programs were established or expanded in agriculture, transportation, natural resources, and other domestic policy areas. These programs, usually funded by annual appropriations and therefore categorized as discretionary, provided the most serious competition for defense through the 1950s.[9]

Second, the New Deal introduced federal social welfare programs, such as social security and public assistance. Most federal social welfare programs operate as entitlements, with spending mandated by law, and the budgetary impact of

TABLE 1. *The framework of post-World War II defense budgeting*

PRESIDENTIAL DEFENSE POLICY (1945-1965)

Demobilization (1945-1950)

Strategic Context:	Uncertainty
Institutional Context:	Presidential Dominance
Budgetary Context:	Domestic Transfers
	Deficit Control

Buildup and Stabilization (1950-1965)

Strategic Context:	Consensus
Institutional Context:	Presidential Dominance
Budgetary Context:	Defense Stabilization
	Deficit Control
	Domestic Transfers

POLITICIZED DEFENSE POLICY (1965-2000+)

Vietnam Transition (1965-1970)

Strategic Context:	Consensus
Institutional Context:	Presidential Dominance
Budgetary Context:	Defense Growth
	Domestic Growth

Post-Vietnam Cuts (1970-1980)

Strategic Context:	Dissensus
Institutional Context:	Congressional Challenges
Budgetary Context:	Domestic Transfers

Reagan Buildup (1980-1990)

Strategic Context:	Consensus
Institutional Context:	Congressional Challenges
Budgetary Context:	Defense Growth
	Domestic Growth

Post-Cold War Cuts (1990-2000+)

Strategic Context:	Uncertainty
Institutional Context:	Congressional Challenges
Budgetary Context:	Domestic Transfers
	Deficit Control

Source: Compiled by author

entitlements has grown enormously over the past three decades.[10] In the early 1960s, entitlements and other mandatory spending were less than one-third of the federal budget, compared to about one-half for defense.[11] Entitlements now account for well over one-half of all federal spending, and their projected growth cannot be accommodated without major reductions in discretionary spending, most notably defense.[12]

These two categories of federal domestic programs have largely defined the budgetary context within which post-World War II defense spending needs have been determined. It has been difficult to stabilize defense funding against competing domestic needs for long periods of time, and the transition from a presidentially dominated defense policymaking process to a more politicized process has worsened the defense budget's competitive disadvantage.

Presidential Defense Policy

By the late 1940s, policymakers had concluded that the United States would be forced to maintain a large military establishment for an indefinite period of time. Over the next two decades, defense spending dominated the federal budget, but defense budgets (and defense policy) did not generate the intense political conflicts now considered routine. Instead, the president was accorded considerable discretion in defining national security needs, and congressional review of the defense budget was, by recent standards, straightforward.[13]

During this period, the executive branch controlled the defense budgetary process and also exercised the concomitant responsibility for integrating defense needs with other budget policy requirements. While steep defense cuts were instituted immediately after World War II, defense spending was then increased and subsequently stabilized at a relatively high level (table 2). Underlying this stability was a national security policy consensus that accorded defense a privileged position in the competition for funds.[14]

TABLE 2. *National defense outlays, fiscal years 1945-1965 (in billions of dollars)*

Fiscal Year	Constant FY 1982 Dollars	Percentage of Total Outlays	Percentage of GNP
1945	$591.3	89.5%	39.1%
1946	339.8	77.3	20.0
1947	89.9	37.1	5.7
1948	55.8	30.6	3.7
1949	77.4	33.9	5.0
1950	83.9	32.2	5.1
1951	150.3	51.8	7.5
1952	258.9	68.1	13.5
1953	271.5	69.4	14.4
1954	250.0	69.5	13.3
1955	211.0	62.4	11.1
1956	198.5	60.2	10.2
1957	203.5	59.3	10.3
1958	198.3	56.8	10.4
1959	196.0	53.2	10.2
1960	192.1	52.2	9.5
1961	195.2	50.8	9.6
1962	202.2	49.0	9.4
1963	197.1	48.0	9.1
1964	198.8	46.2	8.7
1965	181.4	42.8	7.5

Source: *Historical Tables, Budget of the United States Government, Fiscal Year 1992, Part Seven* (Washington, DC: GPO, 1991), 66-68.

Post-World War II Demobilization

Once World War II ended, U.S. force levels and defense budgets plummeted. By fiscal year 1948, real defense outlays had dropped to less than 10 percent of their World War II peak and to what remains their lowest level of the past half-century. The precipitous defense reduction after World War II was fueled by public demands for rapid demobilization, and it drew additional impetus from what the first Secretary of Defense, James V. Forrestal, criticized as strategic naivete:

> We scrapped our war machine, mightiest in the history of the world, in a manifestation of confidence that we should not need it any longer. Our quick and complete demobilization was a testimonial to our good will rather than to our common sense. International frictions which constitute a threat to our national security and to the peace of the world have since compelled us to strengthen our armed forces for self-protection.[15]

Fiscal policy considerations also affected defense. The Truman administration was determined to check inflationary pressures through deficit control and succeeded in balancing three consecutive budgets, a record unmatched by any of its successors. The fiscal year 1948 surplus of nearly $12 billion, when defense was at its nadir, remains the largest in U.S. history.

President Truman's focus on deficit control translated into tight spending limits for defense. Outlay-GNP levels during the late 1940s averaged less than 15 percent, compared to current levels of well over 20 percent. Because Truman was also committed to expanding domestic spending, tradeoffs from defense to domestic spending were inevitable. These tradeoffs allowed Truman to control deficits, while tripling the nondefense share of the budget.

The Truman administration's budget program remained in place up to the outbreak of the Korean War, despite its sponsorship of a containment doctrine that called for a more aggressive U.S. national security policy. As one recent study concluded, the containment doctrine's "profound" intellectual implications had "almost no immediate impact on the level of military preparedness. Truman's rigid insistence on balancing the budget . . . kept a tight lid on military spending until the attack on South Korea in June 1950."[16]

In Truman's fiscal year 1950 budget message, the administration's defense request was characterized as a "position of relative military readiness" that could be maintained at similar levels for the "foreseeable future."[17] One year later, the administration's defense request was reduced by nearly 10 percent. According to Truman, this reduction was consistent with "a balanced structure which can be maintained over a period of years without an undue use of national resources."[18]

Congress was likewise reluctant to support high levels of military preparedness. While clashing with the administration over interservice funding allocations, particularly for the Navy and Air Force, Congress was in agreement that military budgets should be tightly controlled. After cutting the fiscal 1950 defense appropriations bill by over $1 billion, the Senate Appropriations Committee warned that "a nation which exhausts itself in enervating overpreparation . . . may well fall prey to a cunning and patient enemy who fully realizes the debilitating influences of a war-geared economy over a long period of time."[19]

The growing disparity between strategic requirements and defense budgets was finally resolved with the outbreak of war in Korea. The buildup that followed included major expansions of conventional and strategic forces unrelated to the Korean conflict. Defense outlays quadrupled between FY 1950 and FY 1953, the defense budget share rose to nearly 70 percent, and the defense-GNP level climbed to nearly 15 percent. Much of the growth in the defense budget was devoted to capital investment programs, such as procurement, military construction, and atomic energy defense programs.[20] The extent of Truman's defense policy reversal was apparent in his final budget submission to Congress, which called for maintaining peacetime defense spending "in the neighborhood of 35 to 40 billion dollars annually."[21] This was roughly three times as high as average annual outlays for the fiscal 1947-

1950 period.

While the incoming Eisenhower administration began almost immediately to reduce Truman's defense budget projections, nothing approaching the post-World War II defense cutback was repeated after Korea. Defense spending during the Korean conflict never matched World War II levels, but postwar defense budgets remained much higher after Korea. The span between Korea and Vietnam represents a rare stabilization in peacetime defense spending, with defense drawing political support from a bipartisan strategic consensus and from the concomitant perception that U.S. military weaknesses might have contributed to the Korean War's outbreak:

> Had Truman not been myopically focused on a balanced budget, he might have avoided the Korean War, for military stringency lay at the root of Secretary of State Dean Acheson's carefully considered policy speech on January 12, 1950, which tempted fate by defining the U.S. defense perimeter in Asia to exclude Korea and Formosa.[22]

Defense Stabilization

Between the end of the Korean War and the beginning of the Vietnam War, defense spending remained the single largest component of the federal budget, accounting for about one-half of total outlays. Over this period, real defense spending averaged approximately $200 billion annually (in FY 1982 dollars), nearly 75 percent of its Korean War peak. Although real growth in the overall budget was reserved for domestic programs, the large defense budget share limited domestic program expansions. Efforts by the Johnson administration to ease these limits by sharply cutting defense were interrupted by the Vietnam War, but Johnson's commitment to domestic program increases continued even as wartime spending escalated and presaged future efforts to redirect budget policy.

The New Look. The Eisenhower administration, like its predecessor, was strongly committed to balanced budgets. According to Iwan W. Morgan, "From the very beginning of his presidency, Eisenhower's conduct of national security policy was guided by a sense of the economic limits of American military power."[23] For Eisenhower, this concern with the fiscal and budgetary impact of large defense budgets was reinforced by doubts that the country could support "so-called adequate defense over a sustained period without drastically changing [its] whole way of life."[24]

Eisenhower's defense program, christened the "New Look," substituted strategic force expansions for manpower and conventional forces. Military manpower levels declined by nearly one-third, to 2.5 million in 1960, from their Korean War peak, and defense budgets were geared toward missiles and airpower. Between fiscal years 1955 and 1960, procurement outlays for missiles rose from $631 million to $3.8 billion.[25] In fiscal year 1960, the Air Force's budget was nearly equal to the combined budgets of the Navy and Army; 10 years earlier, the Air Force had received the smallest of the service budgets.[26]

The centerpiece of Eisenhower's defense budget strategy was the deterrent concept of massive retaliation, with the United States relying upon nuclear weapons to deter Soviet aggression. In Europe, the United States rejected as too costly the conventional force buildups necessary to achieve parity with Warsaw Pact forces, declaring instead that "atomic weapons in substantial quantities would be available for the support of its presently programmed forces."[27] Since strategic forces were much cheaper than conventional forces, the massive retaliation doctrine permitted the Eisenhower administration to control defense budgets without overtly sacrificing strategic planning requirements.

While much criticism was directed toward the massive retaliation doctrine, the predominant congressional critique was that too little was being spent on defense. In order to fund conventional as well as strategic force improvements, Congress constantly pressed for higher defense ceilings, but usually settled for funding defense budgets at requested levels. For peacetime defense budgets covering fiscal years 1955-1961, enacted budget authority ($287.6 billion) and recommended budget authority ($289.6) differed by less than 1 percent.[28] Congress challenged, often heatedly, the allocations of funds among the services and their programs, but the administration usually prevailed. Moreover, the interservice competition for funds in Congress had as its general aim the raising of overall defense budgets rather than the redirecting of funds within lower ceilings.

The 1960 presidential election featured sharp partisan attacks on the "missile gap, space gap, limited-war gap" that Democrats charged had resulted from "lack of budgetary support."[29] Despite defense spending levels already in place that accounted for nearly one-half of the budget and almost 10 percent of GNP, John F. Kennedy pledged to increase funding for a broad range of forces. As it turned out, the post-election defense increases were modest and short-lived, as competing domestic program needs soon emerged. Eisenhower had, in fact, been remarkably prescient in his insistence on budget ceilings or "directed verdicts" to stabilize and protect defense budgets.

Flexible Response. The Kennedy administration's initial budget program called for defense budget increases to support its new "flexible response" doctrine. Additional funding was sought for strategic programs, conventional forces, and also for the limited-war capabilities that would provide the broad range of force options constituting flexible response. According to the Kennedy administration, its defense program was decidedly more costly than Eisenhower's. President Kennedy's fiscal 1963 budget message, for example, claimed that defense outlays were $9 billion higher for fiscal years 1962 and 1963, and budget authority levels $12 to $15 billion greater, than would have been required under the Eisenhower defense program.[30]

Disputes with the Soviets over Berlin in 1961 and Cuba in 1962 added urgency to Kennedy's defense buildup. Three months after the Cuban missile crisis, the administration's fiscal 1964 budget was submitted to Congress, with Kennedy announcing that "there is no discount price for defense."[31] While Kennedy's language suggested that defense budgets would continue to rise, budget policy planning was already shifting to domestic program support. The fiscal 1965 budget, submitted by Lyndon B. Johnson just 2 months after the Kennedy assassination, called for an $800 million cut in defense outlays. Johnson asserted that stepped-up military spending over the preceding 3 years had created "the most formidable defense establishment the world has ever known," including strategic forces that were "vastly superior to the Soviet nuclear force."[32]

Defense spending during fiscal year 1965 dropped much more rapidly than Johnson had estimated. Actual FY 1965 outlays were almost $4 billion below FY 1964 levels, while real defense spending, the defense budget share, and the defense-GNP share declined to their lowest levels since the Korean buildup. Indeed, on each of these dimensions, peacetime defense budgets under Kennedy and Johnson were lower than Eisenhower's (table 3).

TABLE 3. *Peacetime defense budget comparisons, Eisenhower and Kennedy-Johnson administrations (in billions of dollars)*

	Average Annual Level		
Fiscal Year	Constant (FY 1982) Dollars	Percentage of Total Outlays	Percentage of GNP
1955-1960 (Eisenhower)	$199.9	57.3%	10.3%
1961-1965 (Kennedy-Johnson)	194.9	47.4	8.9

Source: *Historical Tables, Budget of the United States Government, Fiscal Year 1992, Part Seven* (Washington, DC: GPO, 1991), 67-68.

There was an additional distinction between the Eisenhower and Kennedy-Johnson budget programs. Defense spending limits under Eisenhower were based upon economic impact and sustainability, while the Kennedy-Johnson defense program had a short-term political focus. After a temporary surge in defense spending, primarily for programs initiated by Eisenhower, attention shifted to domestic program support. With defense absorbing over 40 percent of the budget even after the fiscal 1965 reductions, the margin to support other programs remained small. Attempts to widen that margin were stymied, albeit temporarily, by Vietnam.

Politicized Defense Policy

The Vietnam War radically altered the defense budgetary process. Partisan and ideological differences in Congress over defense policy and defense budgets widened significantly. Relations between Congress and the executive branch became highly confrontational, as procedural requirements for defense authorizations and appropriations were tightened and congressional oversight on defense policy matters was expanded. Finally, in 1974, Congress attempted to integrate defense spending into a new congressional budget process. As described by Blechman, "For the first time in its history, [Congress] began to play an active role in shaping the structure of U.S. military forces. Through countless amendments to various budgetary vehicles, the Congress sought to shift priorities in U.S. defense planning and to alter the disposition and characteristics of U.S. military forces."[33]

The Vietnam Transition

In terms of defense budgeting, the Vietnam War had two stages. During the first stage, which lasted approximately from 1965 through the spring of 1968, Congress not only provided strong support for U.S. intervention but repeatedly insisted that non-Vietnam defense needs not be slighted. During the second stage, which began in 1969 and continued for the next four years, Congress reversed course on both the war and the overall military budget, moving to cut defense budgets and to transfer funding to domestic programs. That this occurred during wartime was highly unusual, but the funding pattern for Vietnam had, in fact, been unusual from the outset.

The Johnson Presidency. After his landslide victory in the 1964 presidential election, Lyndon B. Johnson was ready to implement the most ambitious domestic agenda since the New Deal. On the spending side, Johnson pledged to redirect funds from defense to domestic programs in order "to grasp the opportunities of the Great Society."[34] Johnson's fiscal year 1966 budget also declared that "the ratio of federal spending to our total output will continue to decline."[35] Under the administration's fiscal plan, balanced budgets were to be achieved through spending control, not tax increases, necessitating even sharper defense cuts to fund Johnson's domestic initiatives.

As the Vietnam commitment deepened, defense spending rose sharply, but Johnson resisted offsetting reductions in his domestic budget program. Domestic outlays were allowed to rise along with wartime defense spending, while major tax increases were repeatedly postponed. Neither spending nor tax policy during Vietnam paralleled the financing patterns during World War II and Korea, when revenue levels were raised sharply and nondefense spending levels were cut. During Korea, for example, real defense outlays rose to over $270 billion and the defense share of total outlays more than doubled, to nearly 70 percent. During Vietnam, while real defense outlays climbed close to the Korean War levels, the defense budget share remained well under 50 percent (table 4).

The Johnson administration's refusal to subordinate its domestic policy agenda, and its repeated underestimates of Vietnam-related spending, led congressional military supporters to demand postwar defense budget increases in order to buttress capabilities that had been neglected.[36] In January 1968, congressional leaders were reassured by Johnson's new Secretary of Defense, Clark M. Clifford, that the U.S. would no longer settle for nuclear arms parity with the Soviet Union but would instead seek outright superiority.[37] Later that year, Senate Armed Services Committee chairman Richard B. Russell announced that "we cannot continue to support a war, be capable of honoring our commitments abroad, and maintain an adequate defense posture without

17

TABLE 4. *Defense and nondefense outlays, fiscal years 1965-1969 (in billions of dollars)*

	Fiscal Year				
	1965	1966	1967	1968	1969
	Constant FY 1982 Dollar Outlays				
Defense	$181.4	$197.9	$235.1	$254.8	$243.4
Nondefense	213.2	233.3	253.4	270.7	266.9
	Percentage of Total Outlays				
Defense	42.8%	43.2%	45.4%	46.0%	44.9%
Nondefense	57.2	56.8	54.6	54.0	55.1
	Percentage of GNP				
Defense	7.5%	7.9%	9.0%	9.6%	8.9%
Nondefense	10.1	10.3	10.8	11.3	10.9

Source: *Historical Tables, Budget of the United States Government, Fiscal Year 1992, Part Seven* (Washington, DC: GPO, 1991), 68.

substantially increasing the size of our defense budget in the near future. As reluctant as Congress will be to accept that statement, I make it unequivocally and without fear of contradiction."[38]

The Political Balance. The political support for defense, however, had declined as opposition to the war had increased. Public support for defense spending, which had been strong during the 1950s and early 1960s, plummeted during the late 1960s. According to Russett, "The cumulative impact of the Vietnam war produced an aversion to things military, so that by the beginning of the 1970s only a fifth of the population wanted to spend more on defense and half the population wanted to spend less."[39] Congressional decisions about defense spending mirrored this public opinion shift.[40] Congress was no longer pressing for more weapons systems and balanced forces, as it had prior to and during the early stages of Vietnam, but instead was demanding that defense budgets be cut and domestic spending increased.

The bipartisan consensus on defense policy was shattered by Vietnam, and the Great Society had introduced a host of domestic programs ready to benefit from defense's diminished political support. Domestic transfer pressures had been building in Johnson's pre-Vietnam budgets. By the end of the decade, these pressures had intensified, and the budget outlook for defense was deteriorating.

Post-Vietnam Cuts

The 1968 Republican platform had decried the Johnson administration's defense record, declaring, "We have frittered away superior military capabilities, enabling the Soviets to narrow their defense gap, in some areas to outstrip us, and to move to cancel our lead entirely by the early Seventies."[41] Richard M. Nixon's presidential election victory, however, did little to check the growing public and congressional demands for defense budget cuts. Variously described as the "peace dividend," "peace and growth dividend," "fiscal dividend," and "budgetary gap," post-Vietnam defense reductions estimated at up to $40 billion per year were being claimed for domestic program support.[42] While the more extravagant peace dividend claims proved illusory, a pronounced shift from defense to domestic programs did occur.

The Nixon-Ford Presidencies. Beginning in fiscal year 1969, real defense outlays started to decline and, by the end of the Nixon-Ford administrations, had dropped 25 percent below pre-Vietnam levels. The defense budget share and defense GNP share dropped sharply as well, with both declining to pre-Korea levels. At the same time, nondefense spending skyrocketed (table 5). Over the fiscal year 1969-1977 period, for example, nondefense outlays increased by over $200 billion, or approximately 75 percent, while total federal spending as a percentage of GNP climbed to its highest level since World War II.[43] The size of the budget relative to the economy was comparable to the Korean and Vietnam wartime levels, although the defense component was much lower.

The Nixon administration attempted, with only limited success, to cushion defense from congressional cuts. Management reforms were implemented within the Department of Defense, and strategic and force doctrines were modified in line with budgetary constraints. The Nixon Doctrine, announced in 1969, declared that other nations would need to contribute significantly to collective defense. In 1970, the Nixon Doctrine was extended to include a "one-and-a-half war" planning strategy for the armed forces, compared to the "two-and-a-half wars" under Johnson. Nixon also resumed arms control negotiations with the Soviets and committed his administration to an all-volunteer military, in order to defuse antidefense critiques.

By the end of Nixon's first term, the Vietnam War was in its final stages, and Nixon was aggressively challenging Congress on the future direction of budget policy. Earlier in the year, Nixon had warned Congress against "the dangerous course of trying to match domestic spending increases with cuts in vitally needed defense programs."[44] The 1972 presidential campaign, which featured a Democratic plan calling for a one-third defense cut over 3 years in order to supply funds for "programs of direct and immediate benefit to our people," allowed Nixon to step up the attack on the Democratic party as antidefense.[45] Nixon's budget policy goal was to protect defense spending and, at the same time, to reduce or eliminate a wide range of domestic spending programs.

Nixon's overwhelming reelection victory allowed him to intensify his battle with Congress over budget ceilings, domestic spending vetoes, and presidential impoundments of appropriated funds. Nixon used these budget policy disputes to buttress a full-scale indictment of the congressional budgetary process, and, for the first part of 1973, Nixon's assault placed Congress on the defensive. As the Watergate scandal unfolded, however, Nixon's political leverage

TABLE 5. *Defense and nondefense outlays, fiscal years 1969-1977 (in billions of dollars)*

Fiscal Year	Constant (FY 1982) Dollars		Percentage of Total Outlays		Percentage of GNP	
	Defense	Nondefense	Defense	Nondefense	Defense	Nondefense
1969	$243.4	$266.9	44.9%	55.1%	8.9%	10.9%
1970	225.6	283.7	41.8	58.2	8.3	11.5
1971	202.7	306.7	37.5	62.5	7.5	12.4
1972	190.9	336.7	34.3	65.7	6.9	13.1
1973	175.1	352.4	31.2	68.8	6.0	13.2
1974	163.3	365.3	29.5	70.5	5.6	13.4
1975	159.8	426.2	26.0	74.0	5.7	16.1
1976	153.6	456.2	24.1	75.9	5.3	16.6
1977	154.3	468.3	23.8	76.2	5.0	16.1

Source: *Historical Tables, Budget of the United States Government, Fiscal Year 1992, Part Seven* (Washington, DC: GPO, 1991), 68-69

disappeared, and his attacks against congressional spending prerogatives abruptly ended. The administration's fiscal year 1975 budget was a marked departure from the previous year's aggressive document, essentially conceding the domestic spending agenda to Congress.

Gerald Ford, who succeeded Nixon on August 9, 1974, attempted to renew the budget policy battles with Congress but with little success. Over the first several months of his administration, Ford suffered four veto overrides, and the new Congress he faced in 1975 was even more heavily Democratic than its predecessor. Included among its early rebuffs to Ford were a cut of $7.3 billion in the president's fiscal year 1976 defense budget request, rejection of $5 billion in proposed domestic program reductions, and appropriations add-ons of more than $3 billion on nondefense spending bills.[46]

President Ford renewed the fight for higher defense budgets the following year. His case was strengthened by mounting evidence of unfavorable force comparisons between the U.S. and the Soviet Union, including a Congressional Research Service (CRS) study that characterized the shortcomings in U.S. capabilities as severe and concluded that "U.S. budgetary projections paint a bleak picture when related to pressing U.S. problems, even though absolute outlays are very large."[47] Public opinion was also shifting in favor of higher defense budgets, with perceptions of the Soviet threat becoming increasingly pessimistic.[48] With these assessments by the general public and by policy experts serving to broaden political support for defense, the decline in real defense outlays was finally halted, but there was no marked reversal in budget policy, and the defense share of the budget continued to shrink.

The Carter Years. While real defense outlays rose during each year of Jimmy Carter's presidency, defense growth was extremely limited, particularly in comparison to strategic requirements. For the first 2 years of his administration, Carter joined Congress in continuing the domestic spending expansion of prior years but coupled this to "prudent real growth" in defense.[49] Prudence in this context was defined as "considerably more moderate than . . . the previous administration."[50] Prudence also meant that while defense cuts would no longer be used to fund nondefense programs, defense budget growth would lag well behind the rest of the budget.

During the latter part of Carter's tenure, defense was assigned a higher priority. In 1979, Carter proposed a 3 percent real growth target for defense. Later in the year, after the seizure of U.S. embassy personnel in Iran had crystallized latent public fears about U.S. military weakness, Carter nearly doubled his long-term growth targets for defense. The Soviet Union's invasion of Afghanistan, on December 29, 1979, then touched off a bidding war on defense that soon found Congress forcing the administration to increase yet again its defense budget requests.

The budget policy indecisiveness of the Carter years was acute. According to the administration's own diagnoses, the defense budget was seriously deficient, but the administration and Congress were unwilling to sacrifice other budget policy goals to accommodate defense. The 1980 report of Secretary of Defense Harold Brown conceded that "relative defense spending, annual or cumulative, is the best single crude measure of relative military capabilities" and estimated that, by this measure, the Soviet funding advantage over the United States was between 25 and 45 percent.[51] Measured against disparities of this magnitude, the pace of budgetary change under Carter could only be described as anemic (table 6). Even after the upward adjustment in Carter's defense requests, defense budget shares remained at their lowest levels since before World War II.

The budget policy debates of the Carter years were intensely ideological, despite Democratic control of the White House and Congress. Congressional budget resolutions served as lightning rods for passionate, if ofttimes symbolic, debates over defense and domestic needs, straining relations between the administration and Congress and continually delaying action on authorization and appropriations bills. The heightened politicization of defense policy did not end with the priority-setting battles over congressional budget resolutions. Instead, the annual defense authorization and defense appropriations

TABLE 6. *Defense and nondefense outlays, fiscal years 1977-1981 (in billions of dollars)*

	Fiscal Year				
	1977	1978	1979	1980	1981
	Constant FY 1982 Dollar Outlays				
Defense	$154.3	$155.0	$159.1	$164.0	$171.4
Nondefense	468.3	497.1	501.0	535.1	555.2
	Percentage of Total Outlays				
Defense	23.8%	22.8%	23.1%	22.7%	23.2%
Nondefense	76.2	77.2	76.9	77.3	76.8
	Percentage of GNP				
Defense	5.0%	4.8%	4.8%	5.0%	5.3%
Nondefense	16.1	16.3	5.8	17.1	17.4

Source: *Historical Tables, Budget of the United States Government, Fiscal Year 1992, Part Seven* (Washington, DC: GPO, 1991), 69.

bills served as vehicles for renewing funding fights that had been previously lost and for imposing additional controls on the internal operations of the Department of Defense.

Hearings at each of the three stages of the defense budget process in Congress—budget resolutions, authorizations, and appropriations—grew in length and detail.[52] The number of committees and subcommittees claiming jurisdiction over defense policy increased. Floor debates were prolonged and heated, floor amendments to defense bills proliferated, and highly specific policy directives became routine. Line-item authorizations and appropriations, aimed at strictly delimiting spending authority for the Department of Defense, became more and more frequent. By the end of the Carter presidency, line-item authorization had been extended to 70 percent of the defense budget, compared to 3 percent after World War II.[53] (Under Reagan and Bush, the total continued to climb, reaching 100 percent by the early 1990s.)[54]

The political and procedural complexity of the defense budget process during the late 1970s made it even more difficult to define and implement a coherent defense strategy. Weakened by events and perceptions it could not control, the Carter administration was further hamstrung in its efforts to forge a post-Vietnam defense consensus by an aggressive Congress that refused to follow but was incapable of leading. In the absence of consistent and committed presidential leadership, it proved impossible to reestablish a strategic consensus that could insulate defense budgets from the narrow, short-term focus of annual budget policy debates in Congress.

According to the Carter administration, defense funding had to increase to strengthen essential military capabilities. Congressional defense experts concurred in this assessment, but no agreement could be reached on a budget program to implement the necessary buildup. By the end of the Carter presidency, defense levels were still low, tax levels were relatively high, and deficits were climbing.[55] Against this backdrop, the administration's liberal critics in Congress charged that domestic needs were being neglected. Carter's attempt to avoid divisive budget policy battles had increased rather than defused controversy and crippled his presidency.

The Reagan Buildup

When Ronald Reagan took office, he immediately increased Carter's defense spending program, proposing a 5-year plan to raise the defense budget share by over 60 percent and the defense GNP share by more than 30 percent.[56] While Reagan was unable to shift budget policy quite this dramatically, he did succeed in raising real defense spending levels quickly and significantly (table 7). By the end of the Reagan presidency, and despite large and repeated congressional cuts in Reagan's defense budget requests, real defense spending had risen to

Korean and Vietnam War peak levels.[57]

The Reagan defense program provided additional funding for all of the major categories of the defense budget, while targeting investment accounts (notably procurement and research and development) and strategic force modernization for especially large increases. During the administration's first term, budget authority increases for investment accounts were more than double the rate of growth for the remainder of the defense budget. Strategic force funding was programmed for higher growth than other mission categories, with the administration describing its plan as "the greatest addition of modern, strengthened strategic forces planned and funded by any United States President."[58]

Defense Policy. This reorientation of the defense budget was a response to the widely acknowledged long-term funding deficiencies in procurement programs. The Carter administration had proposed boosting the investment share of defense spending and modernizing strategic forces, but its funding shifts were minor compared to the Reagan program. Over the fiscal year 1980-1982 period, Carter's defense planners had proposed increasing the investment share of the defense budget from 36 percent to 38 percent.[59] Reagan's defense budgets raised the investment share to 42 percent for fiscal year 1982 and to 46 percent for fiscal year 1983.[60] Since the Reagan defense budgets were considerably larger than Carter's, the impact on military capabilities was magnified.

In addition to immediate outlay increases across the entire defense budget, the Reagan buildup included multiyear investment budget authority commitments that locked in long-term defense spending increases. Over Reagan's first term, procurement budget authority more than doubled, from $48.0 billion in FY 1981 to $96.8 billion in FY 1985. Over the fiscal year 1985-1989 period, when new procurement budget authority was reduced by almost 20 percent, the backlog of programs for which funding had already been approved helped to raise actual procurement spending by roughly the same amount.

The Reagan defense program did not alter basic U.S. strategy, although the Strategic Defense Initiative that Reagan

TABLE 7. *Defense and nondefense outlays, fiscal years 1981-1989 (in billions of dollars)*

Fiscal Year	Constant (FY 1982) Dollars		Percentage of Total Outlays		Percentage of GNP	
	Defense	Nondefense	Defense	Nondefense	Defense	Nondefense
1981	$171.4	$555.2	23.2%	76.8%	5.3%	17.4%
1982	185.3	560.4	24.9	75.1	5.9	17.9
1983	201.3	573.7	26.0	74.0	6.3	18.0
1984	211.3	576.8	26.7	73.3	6.2	16.9
1985	230.0	619.8	26.7	73.3	6.4	17.5
1986	244.0	624.0	27.6	72.4	6.5	17.1
1987	251.0	607.4	28.1	71.9	6.4	16.3
1988	252.8	627.9	27.3	72.7	6.1	16.2
1989	256.6	653.0	26.5	73.5	5.9	16.4

Source: *Historical Tables, Budget of the United States Government, Fiscal Year 1992, Part Seven* (Washington, DC: GPO, 1991), 69-70.

unveiled in 1983 represented a potentially major change. At the level of specific weapons systems, the transition from Carter to Reagan was largely one of scale. With the exception of Reagan's support for the B-1 bomber and for large nuclear-powered aircraft carriers, there were few differences between the weapons programs of the two administrations, but Reagan substantially raised procurement levels and speeded up procurement timetables. The Carter administration's 5-year shipbuilding program, for example, was increased by 50 percent, and its naval budgets were raised by an even greater amount.[61] A similar pattern of comprehensive upward revision applied to research and development programs.

The Reagan administration repeatedly clashed with Congress over weapons systems, arms control, strategic force modernization, and other elements of defense policy. Congress used defense spending bills as vehicles for attacking the administration's management of the Department of Defense and for criticizing the administration's handling of national security policy and foreign policy, but these were part of an even broader disagreement over the Reagan administration's defense budget strategy. With Reagan insisting that the size of the defense budget measured not just military strength but also commitment and will, budget numbers dominated defense policy debates. Reagan's willingness to fight for the highest possible numbers, even as deficits mounted to unprecedented levels, provided the presidential leadership that previously had been lacking in defense policy debates, and the unfavorable U.S.-Soviet force comparisons that had emerged during the 1970s supplied Reagan with a strategic rationale for increasing the pressure on Congress. The defense budget process was no less politicized than it had been during the 1970s, but the Reagan administration used this politicization to its advantage, at least during its first term.

Budget Policy. The Reagan administration's initial economic planning claimed that tax cuts and defense increases could be integrated into a balanced budget program through offsetting domestic spending reductions. In 1981, Reagan was able to push through Congress the Omnibus Budget Reconciliation Act of 1981 that reduced or eliminated a substantial number of domestic programs, including some entitlements. A second round of administration-sponsored cuts later in the year was rejected by Congress, with the ensuing stalemate continuing for the remainder of Reagan's tenure. Reagan was able to block the growth of discretionary domestic spending programs, but entitlement levels remained high, and net interest outlays rose sharply. Thus, while total discretionary spending as a percentage of GNP declined during the 1980s—albeit shifting in emphasis from domestic to defense spending—the relative level of total federal spending actually increased.

The Reagan tax program included structural tax reform, as well as marginal rate reductions and other tax cuts. Despite the cuts, most notably the 1981 Economic Recovery Tax Act, revenue levels under Reagan were actually slightly higher than the averages during the 1960s and 1970s. Because spending levels were much higher during the 1980s, however, deficits rose very sharply (table 8). The great budgetary impasse between the Reagan administration and Congress was rooted in the intractability of these large structural deficits.

Because the relatively high spending levels during Reagan's presidency were attributable primarily to entitlements, the administration was unable to bring spending down to revenue levels. Conversely, the administration was unalterably opposed to raising revenue levels anywhere near spending. By Reagan's second term, deficit control and domestic transfer pressures were making it more and more difficult to sustain the defense buildup. Public support for defense increases had waned.[62] Congress was returning to its earlier practice of trying to finance domestic program increases with defense cuts, while the administration was unwilling to trade tax increases for defense increases. With first-term deficits having averaged nearly $150 billion annually, the stage was set for a decisive encounter between the administration and Congress on budget policy choices.

Instead, both sides finally compromised upon a deficit-reduction procedure that exempted tax policy and most entitlements. The Gramm-Rudman-Hollings bills of 1985

TABLE 8. *Revenues, spending, and deficits, fiscal years 1960-1989 (as percentages of GNP)*

Fiscal Year	Revenues	Average Annual Level Outlays	Deficits
1960-69	18.2%	19.0%	0.8%
1970-79	18.3	20.4	2.1
1980-89	19.0	23.1	4.1

Source: *Historical Tables, Budget of the United States Government, Fiscal Year 1992, Part Seven* (Washington, DC: GPO, 1991), 15.

(GRH I) and 1987 (GRH II) established annual deficit ceilings designed to bring the budget into balance over a 6-year period.[63] If the projected deficit for an upcoming fiscal year was above the ceiling, Congress and the executive branch were required to eliminate the excess deficit through additional taxes or decreased spending. If they failed to do so, automatic spending cuts (sequesters) were to be applied to nonexempt spending programs, essentially defense and discretionary domestic accounts.[64] The cuts between defense and domestic programs were to be apportioned on a roughly 50-50 basis.

For the Reagan administration, the GRH legislation had certain advantages. It insured that any automatic deficit reduction would come solely through spending cuts, thereby protecting Reagan's tax program. The GRH solution removed the immediate pressure on Congress and the executive branch to solve the deficit problem, since the initial GRH ceilings were very generous, and there was little prospect of a significant sequester for several years. The GRH procedures also exempted entitlement programs, which was crucial for the Democratic leadership in Congress. Thus, each side was able to protect its budget policy priorities.

With GRH in place, and congressional resistance having hardened, the defense buildup was essentially finished. Over the fiscal year 1986-1989 period, the average annual difference between Reagan's national defense budget authority requests and enacted budget authority rose to nearly $30 billion. In its FY 1989 defense program, the administration admitted that "Resource constraints have forced us to accept increased risks . . . and a smaller force structure as we strive to preserve required levels of readiness and sustainability."[65]

Defense Budgets and Politics

While the politicization of the defense budget process is usually characterized as a recent, and somewhat aberrant, phenomenon, politicization is rooted in modern budget policy. Peacetime defense funding has typically been volatile, with the only real exception being the period from the end of the Korean War through the early 1960s. Defense's privileged position during this brief period depended upon a strategic consensus and strong presidential leadership, and it came when the domestic budget was at a stage of relative infancy. The New Deal's domestic legacy of social welfare and discretionary domestic programs had enjoyed only a brief peacetime history, and these programs had yet to develop a mature political base of claimants and clientele.

By the mid-1960s, with the Johnson administration nurturing this political base, the prospects for continued stability in defense funding were diminishing rapidly. The Vietnam War's unsatisfactory outcome then provided the opportunity to pursue with a vengeance the funding transfers from defense to domestic programs through which Johnson had planned to build the Great Society. When the adverse effects on national security from these tradeoffs became apparent during the late 1970s, a new, but shaky, consensus emerged for a defense recovery.

The Reagan years supplied enormous real growth but not stability. Some Reagan critics argued that the administration should have pursued slower, sustainable growth rather than the massive first-term push that helped to fuel the second-term congressional reaction. The question is whether Congress could have been relied upon to support a more moderate, sustained program, since, during Reagan's second term, Congress almost immediately reneged on a budget agreement that contained reduced defense growth commitments for fiscal years 1986-1988. It may well be that the budget process in Congress is unalterably short-term in its focus, which suggests the Reagan approach was correct.

The threat to stable defense funding and prudent defense planning is three-fold. In terms of public support, defense will always be disadvantaged in its competition with domestic programs, since the benefits it provides are usually intangible and indirect. In the absence of clear and immediate threats, public support for defense commitments that involve some sacrifice is inherently unreliable, especially when there is no political leadership consensus to shape the public's response.

With public support problematical, congressional incentives multiply to pursue tradeoffs from defense to domestic programs. In addition to the domestic spending benefits thus made available to members of Congress, perennial and wide-open debates on defense budgets allow multiple opportunities for influencing defense policy and weapons systems. Congressional budget policy debates on defense versus nondefense needs may be heavily symbolic, but they legitimize extremely widespread participation by members of Congress on very detailed and specific defense policy issues.

Finally, the evolving shape of the spending budget is disadvantageous to defense. With most of the budget supporting entitlements and mandatory spending, and future growth mortgaged to these programs, the budget policy constraints on defense grow more and more severe, regardless of national security needs. In addition, decreased flexibility in the spending budget renders upward defense adjustments quite difficult.

At the end of the Reagan era, the defense budget was already under considerable pressure because of domestic spending demands and deficit-control efforts. Soon to change as well were the strategic consensus Reagan had strengthened and the presidential commitment he had brought to defense budget debates. As a result, defense has entered into yet another period of instability, the end of which is nowhere in sight.

Notes

1. Before joining the Clinton administration, Panetta served as chairman of the House Budget Committee. House, Committee on the Budget, *Hearing, National Defense Funding and the Fiscal Year 1993 Budget* (Washington, DC: GPO, 1992), 1.

2. According to the Congressional Budget Office, substantial savings have already been incorporated into defense planning. *The Economic and Budget Outlook: Fiscal Years 1993-1997* (Washington, DC: Congressional Budget Office, 1992), 52-55.

3. The tensions between strategic and budgetary considerations are a political fact of life, as explained in a Congressional Research Service study:

Ideally, national security interests are the bases for objectives and commitments which, within policy guidelines, shape strategy. Strategic concepts conditioned by threats generate military force requirements. Budgetary assets then are allocated to satisfy needs. That Utopian sequence rarely occurs in real life. National defense competes with other sectors. There never is enough money to go around. The trick is to walk a tightrope between excessive defense expenditures that emasculate political, economic, social, scientific, and ecological programs on one hand, and deficient defense expenditures that actively endanger national security on the other. Equally important, overallocations in any given military sector can undercut essential capabilities elsewhere.

Congress, Senate, Committee on Armed Services, *United States/ Soviet Military Balance, A Frame of Reference for Congress, A Study by the Library of Congress Congressional Research Service* (Washington, DC: GPO, 1976), 563.

4. In 1992, most federal agencies switched from using gross national product (GNP) to gross domestic product (GDP) as the basic measure of U.S. economic activity. The quantitative differences between the two measures are extremely small, although each has distinctive advantages in terms of economic analysis. During the period covered by this chapter, however, the GNP measure was used exclusively for budget policy purposes, so it has been retained for historically relevant comparisons.

5. Murray Weidenbaum, *Small Wars, Big Defense* (New York: Oxford University Press, 1992), 6.

6. Ibid.

7. See, for example, Barry M. Blechman, *The Politics of National Security* (New York: Oxford University Press, 1990), chap. 2.

8. See Dennis S. Ippolito, *Uncertain Legacies, Federal Budget Policy from Roosevelt through Reagan* (Charlottesville: University Press of Virginia, 1990), 94-98.

9. Discretionary spending includes programs (defense, domestic, and international) funded through appropriations bills. If new appropriations are not enacted, programs cannot be continued. This term is roughly similar to the older description of "relatively controllable under existing law," which was used to designate spending that was contingent upon legislative actions; "relatively uncontrollable" spending, by comparison, could not be increased or decreased without changing existing substantive law. Under the Omnibus Budget Agreement of 1990, spending is divided into five categories: (1) discretionary spending; (2) entitlements and other mandatory spending; (3) deposit insurance; (4) net interest; and (5) offsetting receipts.

10. Once authorization legislation provides for the payment of benefits to recipients meeting legally specified eligibility criteria, these payments (or entitlements) are a binding and legally enforceable obligation on the part of the federal government. Subsequent appropriations are necessary to fund these entitlements. Some appropriations are permanent in duration and indefinite in amount, while others are for limited periods and specific amounts. In neither case, however, is the amount discretionary, since appropriations must cover all of the obligations resulting from prior legislative commitments.

11. *The Economic and Budget Outlook: Fiscal Years 1993-1997*, 119.

12. Ibid., 50.

13. See, for example, Samuel Huntington, *The Soldier and the State* (Cambridge: Harvard University Press, 1957).

14. For a discussion of this "privileged position," see Lawrence J. Korb, *The Fall and Rise of the Pentagon* (Westport, CN.: Greenwood Press, 1979).

15. From Secretary of Defense James V. Forrestal's 1948 report, quoted in *Report of the Secretary of Defense to the President and the Congress* (Washington, DC: GPO, January 1991), x.

16. Townsend Hoopes and Douglas Brinkley, *Driven Patriot, The Life and Times of James Forrestal* (New York: Alfred A. Knopf, 1992), 280.

17. *Congressional Record* 95 (January 10, 1949): 138.

18. *Congressional Record* 96 (January 9, 1950): 214.

19. Quoted in Ippolito, 100.

20. Ibid., 102-03.

21. *Budget of the United States Government, Fiscal Year 1954* (Washington, DC: GPO, 1953), M13.

22. Hoopes and Brinkley, 281. There was the additional, less speculative, concern that defense cutbacks had compromised the readiness of U.S. forces once the Korean War began. This concern was recalled by the chairman of the Joint Chiefs of Staff, General Colin L. Powell, during 1990 congressional hearings on post-Cold War defense funding:

On June 25, 1950, when the North Koreans invaded South Korea, that was a surprise contingency. We had not done a very good job of balancing, shaping, and restructuring our forces in the 5 years since the World War, so our initial response to that contingency was very feeble and cost a lot of blood.

In the absence of a clear threat . . . we had foolishly destroyed our capability to deal with the unexpected. Men died unnecessarily as a result.

Congress, House, Committee on Armed Services, *Hearings, Building a Defense That Works for the Post-Cold War World* (Washington, DC: GPO, 1990), 118.

23. Iwan Morgan, *Eisenhower versus the Spenders* (New York: St. Martin's Press, 1990), 51.

24. *Foreign Relations of the United States, 1952-1954, Vol. 2* (Washington, DC: GPO, 1983), 520. These paraphrased comments were prepared by the National Security Council's Deputy Executive Secretary S. Everett Gleason as part of a discussion memorandum for the Council.

25. Ippolito, 106.

26. Ibid., 107.

27. *Foreign Relations of the United States, 1952-1954, Vol. 5* (Washington, DC: GPO, 1983), 511-12.

28. Ippolito,106.

29. Kirk H. Porter and Donald B. Johnson, eds., *National Party Platforms, 1840-1968* (Urbana: University of Illinois Press, 1970), 575.

30. *Budget of the United States Government, Fiscal Year 1963* (Washington, DC: GPO, 1962), 11.

31. *Budget of the United States Government, Fiscal Year 1964* (Washington, DC: GPO, 1963), 17.

32. *Budget of the United States Government, Fiscal Year 1965* (Washington, DC: GPO, 1964), p 8, 74.

33. Blechman, 11.

34. *Budget of the United States Government, Fiscal Year 1966* (Washington, DC: GPO, 1965), 5.

35. Ibid., 10.

36. See Ippolito, 117-19.

37. *Congress and the Nation, 1965-1968, Vol. II* (Washington, DC: Congressional Quarterly Inc., 1969), 853.

38. Ibid., 830.

39. Bruce Russett, *Controlling the Sword, The Democratic Governance of National Security* (Cambridge: Harvard University Press, 1990), 98.

40. Ibid., 99-100, on the relationship between public opinion and congressional decisionmaking.

41. *Guide to U.S. Elections* (Washington, DC: Congressional Quarterly Inc., 1975), 108.

42. *Congress and the Nation, 1969-1972, Vol. III* (Washington, DC: Congressional Quarterly Inc., 1973), 199.

43. During fiscal years 1976 and 1977, total outlays were just under 22 percent of GNP, approximately 1 percentage point higher than the spending peaks during Korea and Vietnam.

44. *Budget of the United States Government, Fiscal Year 1973* (Washington, DC: GPO, 1972), 15.

45. Ippolito,121-22.

46. *Congressional Quarterly Almanac, 1975* (Washington, DC: Congressional Quarterly Inc., 1976), 764-66.

47. *United States/Soviet Military Balance: A Frame of Reference for Congress,* 32.

48. Ippolito, 126.

49. *Budget of the United States Government, Fiscal Year 1979* (Washington, DC: GPO, 1978), 68.

50. Ibid.

51. *Department of Defense Annual Report, Fiscal Year 1980* (Washington, DC: GPO, 1979), 5.

52. For a general review of these and related changes, see Blechman, chap. 2.

53. John Lehman, *Making War* (New York: Charles Scribner's Sons, 1992), 256.

54. Ibid.

55. During 1980, the congressional Democratic leadership forced the Carter administration to rewrite its fiscal year 1981 budget immediately after it was submitted. House liberals then helped to defeat the new budget plan in the form of a vote on the first concurrent congressional budget resolution. A revised conference version of the first resolution was approved in June, but subsequent action on the second resolution was postponed until after the election. Over the course of the year, Carter's fiscal policies were revised several times, but failed to satisfy Congress or, apparently, the electorate.

56. *Budget Revisions, Fiscal Year 1982* (Washington, DC: GPO, 1981), 11, 125-27.

57. Ippolito, 135, 142.

58. *Department of Defense Annual Report to the Congress, Fiscal Year 1983*, (Washington, DC: GPO, 1982), B-6, I-39.

59. *Department of Defense Annual Report to the Congress, Fiscal Year 1982* (Washington, DC: GPO, 1981), 16, A-1.

60. *Department of Defense Annual Report to the Congress, Fiscal Year 1983* (Washington, DC: GPO, 1984), A-1.

61. Ippolito, 138-40.

62. Ibid., 143.

63. The GRH I timetable called for the budget to be brought into balance over the fiscal year 1986-1991 period. When the sequestration procedure in GRH I was invalidated by the Supreme Court in 1986, a revised procedure was incorporated into GRH II. The GRH II timetable extended the balanced-budget deadline to FY 1993.

64. Social security and other programs, amounting to approximately three-fourths of all domestic spending, were either totally exempt from GRH sequestration or subject to limited cuts. Approximately two-thirds of all military accounts, by comparison, were subject to sequester. See Stanley E. Collender, *The Guide to the Federal Budget, Fiscal 1991* (Washington, DC: The Urban Institute, 1990), 77-80.

65. *Department of Defense Annual Report to the Congress, Fiscal Year 1989*, (Washington, DC: GPO, 1988), 15.

2. Post-Cold War Transition I: The Base Force

THE REPUBLICAN PARTY'S VICTORY in the 1988 presidential election appeared to insure continuity in defense budget policy. During his campaign, George Bush had endorsed the Reagan buildup, pledging to support strategic force modernization and "to correct the dangerous imbalance that now exists in conventional forces."[1] Thus, when Bush took office, many expected the White House to press Congress for increased defense spending.

Contrary to expectations, the defense budget debate was soon transformed. During the first 2 years of the Bush presidency, the Soviet bloc dissolved, and by the end of the third year the Soviet Union had disintegrated. Over this same period, the economic and budget policy outlook in the United States rapidly deteriorated. With the Soviet threat disappearing and budget deficits mounting, the Bush administration attempted to protect defense from abrupt dislocations through a multiyear budget agreement with Congress. The Omnibus Budget Reconciliation Act of 1990, and accompanying Budget Enforcement Act, prohibited spending transfers from defense to domestic programs for 3 years. While the 1990 budget agreement provided short-term protection for the defense budget, its limits on discretionary spending had the unintended effect of making defense more vulnerable to future cuts.

In its insistence that discretionary spending controls would significantly reduce deficits, the Bush administration seriously misdiagnosed the deficit problem. By the late 1980s, neither defense spending in particular nor discretionary spending in general was a major contributor to deficits. Instead, entitlement programs were the primary cause of spending growth and deficit-control problems. When it decided to ignore entitlement program cutbacks and to focus its efforts on discretionary program reductions, the Bush administration was accomplishing very little in terms of deficit reduction and, at the same time, placing long-term defense needs at risk.

In addition, the administration's budget strategy virtually eliminated defense policy as a political issue. Substantive defense policy disagreements between President Bush and Congress were muted in 1991 and 1992, as were budget policy conflicts generally, because of the budget agreement. Even during the 1992 presidential campaign, defense policy issues had little salience. As defense budget planning lost its Cold War framework, partisan differences became blurred, and the link between defense budgets and defense strategy became more tenuous.

Defense and Deficits: 1989

Notwithstanding his campaign rhetoric, President Bush's first defense budget proposals signaled a change in emphasis and approach from the Reagan years. On February 8, 1989, Bush presented his fiscal year 1990 budget program to a joint session of Congress and included defense cutbacks in the administration's deficit-reduction proposals. Bush agreed in "light of the compelling need to reduce the deficit . . . to support a one-year freeze in the military budget."[2] The President stated that "the freeze will apply for only one year—after that, increases above inflation will be required" and invited Congress to negotiate a comprehensive deficit-reduction package.[3]

The 1989 Deficit-Reduction Program

Bush's attempt to link defense cuts to long-term deficit reduction did not succeed. The 1989 budget agreement, which emerged after 2 months of negotiations with congressional Democratic leaders, had no significant impact on overall spending policy or deficits. The administration agreed to cuts in real defense spending but these were offset by increases in discretionary domestic spending. The deficit-reduction provisions finally accepted by Congress were limited to questionable budget-accounting savings, one-time windfalls, and unspecified revenue increases.[4] Most important, entitlement spending was unaffected by the agreement.

The administration's political goal during the 1989 budget talks was to demonstrate its willingness to cooperate with the Democratic-controlled Congress. According to then House Speaker Jim Wright (D-Texas), the executive branch and Congress had accomplished a "very good start in the direction of better cooperation and better performance" even though the budget pact was "not an heroic agreement."[5] Under the circumstances, it was hard to envision how such an agreement could possibly emerge. For Democrats, mandatory spending programs were non-negotiable, even though they accounted for the largest and fastest-growing portion of the budget. For Bush, the "no new taxes" pledge of his campaign apparently precluded significant upward adjustments in tax levels.

The 1989 budget agreement between the Bush administration and Congress was, in intent and in substance, a symbolic exercise. Since no major changes in spending or tax policy had been enacted, the administration could only hope that deficit reduction would be achieved through economic growth and through modest tradeoffs from defense to domestic programs. This hope almost immediately proved to be misplaced. Economic growth during 1990 dropped well below the administration's projections, increasing the FY 1990 budget deficit by approximately $50 billion.[6] Technical estimating errors, primarily for deposit insurance spending, added an additional $50 billion to the deficit.[7] These unanticipated deficit increases greatly exceeded the savings contained in the budget agreement and confirmed the growing irrelevance of discretionary spending controls.

As shown in table 9, actual discretionary spending in FY 1990 was slightly above the levels set in the budget agreement but contributed only a minor amount to the $120+ billion difference between the projected and actual deficits. By comparison, nondiscretionary spending and net interest outlays rose well above projected levels. The deficit was also affected by an emerging economic slowdown that reduced actual revenues below projected levels.

41

The Omnibus Budget Reconciliation Act of 1989

The immediate objective of the 1989 budget agreement was compliance with the deficit-reduction requirements of the Balanced Budget and Emergency Deficit Control Reaffirmation Act of 1987 (the Gramm-Rudman-Hollings statute—GRH II).

TABLE 9. *Fiscal year 1990 budget agreement spending, revenue, and deficit levels versus levels (in billions of dollars)*

Category	Budget Agreement	Actual	Difference
Discretionary spending	$497.5	$501.7	+$4.2
Defense	(299.2)	(300.1)	(0.9)
Domestic	(181.3)	(182.5)	(1.2)
International	(17.0)	(19.1)	(2.1)
Other spending	672.5	750.1	+77.6
Revenues	1,070.6	1,031.3	-39.3
Deficit	99.4	220.5	+121.1

Source: *The Economic and Budget Outlook: Fiscal Years 1993-1997* (Washington, DC: Congressional Budget Office, 1992), 114, 118, 120; *Congressional Quarterly Almanac, 1989* (Washington, DC: Congressional Quarterly Inc., 1990), 85-87.

Under GRH II, the maximum projected deficit for FY 1990 was $100 billion (table 10). Although the 1989 budget agreement contained sufficient deficit-reduction savings to meet the GRH II target, repeated delays in implementing the agreement left the projected deficit above the target when FY 1990 actually began. In order to comply with the GRH II deficit ceiling, President Bush issued a sequestration order on October 16, reducing spending by approximately $16 billion and apportioning half of the cuts to defense and half to domestic programs.[8]

TABLE 10. *Gramm-Rudman-Hollings II maximum deficit amounts and actual deficits, fiscal years 1988-1993 (in billions of dollars)*

Fiscal Year	GRH Maximum	Actual Deficit	Difference
1988	$144	$155	+$ 11
1989	136	153	+ 17
1990	100	221	+ 121
1991	64	270	+ 206
1992	28	290	+ 262
1993 (est.)	0	266	+ 310

*Under GRH II, special deficit-reduction rules applied to fiscal years 1988 and 1989. Deficit targets for fiscal years 1990-1992 could be exceeded by $10 billion before sequestration was triggered. For FY 1993, there were neither special rules nor a deficit cushion.

Source: *The Economic and Budget Outlook: Fiscal Years 1994-1998* (Washington, DC: Congressional Budget Office, 1993), xvi, 124; *The Economic and Budget Outlook: An Update* (Washington, DC: Congressional Budget Office, 1993), 25.

With sequestration in place, the administration and Congress finally concluded action on the implementing legislation for the budget agreement. The Omnibus Budget Reconciliation Act of 1989 (OBRA 1989), which was signed into law on December 19, provided for revenue increases and other savings to meet the GRH II deficit requirement. As part of these savings, OBRA 1989 maintained a portion of the sequestration spending reductions, but these were scaled back to approximately $3.5 billion.[9]

With passage of the 1989 reconciliation bill, the

administration and Congress formally had complied with GRH II, but the sequence of events during 1989 demonstrated both the inadequacies of the GRH II mechanism and the bleak future for deficit reduction. Under GRH II, the deficit target had to be met only once—at the beginning of the fiscal year. Any subsequent deterioration in the deficit outlook, no matter how serious, required no corrective actions.

The spirit of comity that prevailed during the first few months of the Bush presidency soon proved illusory, further complicating the prospects for serious deficit reduction. While the 1989 reconciliation measure had been scheduled for enactment by mid-June, disagreements between the administration and Congress over capital gains tax cuts and a variety of spending program reductions repeatedly stalled final action. The nondefense deficit-reduction provisions that ultimately emerged were restricted to nonrecurring savings, accounting-based reductions, and other transitory actions.[10]

The 1989 budget negotiations did, however, signify an important policy shift from the Reagan years. President Bush was much more willing than his predecessor to subordinate defense spending requirements to a deficit-reduction program and to compromise with Congress on domestic spending.[11] What Bush expected to gain from Congress in making defense negotiable was a moderating of congressional demands to cut defense more sharply, but this approach negated what was, in reality, a crucial policy distinction between a Republican administration and a Democratic Congress. In 1990, when tax policy became negotiable as well, another important policy distinction disappeared.

Defense and Deficits: 1990

The "temporary" defense reductions of 1989 were extended indefinitely the following year. The Bush administration's FY 1991 budget recommended "only slight nominal increases, less than would be required to offset projected inflation" in planning levels for defense.[12] According to the administration, its new defense requests represented 3-year savings of more than $60 billion in budget authority and nearly $30 billion in outlays, when compared to the president's FY 1990 budget program.[13]

Even with these cuts, the administration confronted growing demands for much deeper reductions. Appearing before the Senate Armed Services Committee, Secretary of Defense Richard B. Cheney conceded that the administration's budget was not "a final finished product," while urging Congress to cut the defense budget only "in an intelligent, orderly fashion."[14] Cheney's appeal for caution did not satisfy congressional critics, who sharply attacked the Department of Defense's Soviet threat assessment and related national security planning.

The Soviet Threat Assessment

On December 7, 1988, in a speech to the United Nations, then Soviet President Mikhail Gorbachev had announced unilateral reductions in Soviet force levels and troop withdrawals from Eastern Europe. Four months later, the Soviets had begun to implement their troop withdrawals. By mid-1990, according to estimates compiled by the House Armed Services Committee earlier in the year, approximately half of the Soviet's planned reductions in tanks, aircraft, manpower, and divisions would be completed.[15]

According to some analysts, the Soviet's "new thinking" on national security issues had dramatically diminished the Soviet threat, greatly improving prospects for comprehensive arms control agreements and for conventional force reductions in Europe. In addition, these analysts argued that the Soviet Union's deteriorating economy would preclude a revived Soviet military threat. One dimension of the debate over the U.S. defense budget, therefore, focused upon how to interpret changing Soviet military capabilities and Soviet political intentions.

Members of Congress who found the Bush administration's scaled-down defense planning too costly charged that U.S. "budgets were based on outdated assumptions about the [Soviet] threat, assumptions that reflected inaccurate assessments of what the security environment used to be and ignored what it was becoming."[16] A July 1990 report issued by the Democratic majority on the House Armed Services Committee's Defense Policy Panel concluded that Department of Defense representatives, most notably Secretary Cheney, "[had] been overly cautious, even grudging, in [their] appreciation of how the Soviet threat is changing."[17] Of particular relevance, these Democrats agreed that the debate over the Soviet threat, regardless of its complexity, had to be decided in time to shape the fiscal year 1991 defense budget: "The worst thing we can do is spend too little on defense. The next worst thing we can do is spend too much."[18]

The administration's congressional adversaries were unswayed by evidence of a broad-based Soviet strategic modernization program that, according to Central Intelligence Agency (CIA) Director William H. Webster, was designed to protect and improve "the overall capabilities of their strategic forces."[19] The CIA's strategic force assessment was largely dismissed by House Armed Services Committee Democrats, who countered that strengthened capabilities did not necessarily mean an increased threat. By comparison, the CIA's assessment that the reduction in Soviet conventional capabilities was irreversible was cited as convincing evidence of a permanently reduced threat. For conventional forces, less capability meant less threat, regardless of Soviet intentions. The strategic weapons calculus apparently differed; improved capability meant less threat, because Soviet intentions reduced risk.[20]

Based on this reasoning, the defense budget's prospects were obviously grim. By mid-1990, many in Congress were eager to fashion a new and less menacing version of the Soviet threat that would permit defense budget savings to be realized as quickly as possible. The Bush administration, despite its pleas for caution, faced a Congress in which budgetary considerations demanded immediate strategic reassessments.

The Sequestration Threat Assessment

When its FY 1991 budget was submitted to Congress, the Bush administration reported that the GRH II deficit target would be met without "major legislative" changes.[21] During FY 1991, according to the administration, the deficit would remain within the $64 billion GRH II ceiling even with very limited economic growth.   In addition, the president's budget, purportedly "excluding gimmicks," projected surpluses for fiscal years 1993- 95.[22]

Within a few months, these reassuring deficit projections had been abandoned, and the new deficit estimates were so large that neither the administration nor Congress could, as a practical matter, accept the automatic spending cuts that would be required under GRH II.   The administration's bargaining position on defense became much weaker as the infeasibility of a massive sequestration became more apparent.   Since Congress wanted to cut defense anyway, a small sequestration posed little threat to defense, and with half of any sequestration applying to domestic programs, Congress faced proportional cuts in its favored programs.   The GRH II apportionment formula increased the pressure on Congress to negotiate an alternative to sequestration, but only so long as any threatened sequestration was sufficiently small to be realistic.

In March, the Congressional Budget Office (CBO) projected the FY 1991 deficit under the administration's budget program at over $100 billion and the FY 1991 baseline deficit at over $160 billion.   Since the administration's budget program included deficit-reduction proposals that had little likelihood of enactment, the baseline deficit projection was the more realistic figure.   The Bush administration was therefore facing a sequestration of at least $100 billion for FY 1991, with one-half coming out of the defense budget, and the administration's allies in Congress accordingly began pressing for a budget summit.

On May 6, Bush invited congressional leaders to the White House to propose high-level budget talks.   Three days later, Bush's offer was accepted, and, on May 15, administration and congressional negotiators met in the first of a series of closed-door sessions.   When the budget summit commenced, the projected sequestration for FY 1991 threatened a 27 percent across-the-board cut in defense programs and a 40 percent cut in many domestic programs.[23] As these short-term projections

47

continued to climb, so did the probability of additional, large sequesters to meet the GRH II deficit targets for fiscal years 1992 and 1993.

The potentially huge impact on discretionary spending posed by sequestration was a function of GRH II's unusual budget-balancing mechanism. Since revenues were not part of this mechanism, spending programs had to absorb the entire cost of automatic deficit reduction. Further, only certain types of spending could be sequestered, since many nondefense programs were fully or partially exempt from automatic GRH II cuts.

The sequestration spending exemptions applied to virtually all of the large entitlements. Federal retirement programs, such as social security, railroad retirement, and federal civil and military retirement, were totally exempt from sequestration. Most income assistance programs for the poor (food stamps, aid to families with dependent children, supplemental security income, and medicaid grants to the states) were also nonsequestrable. Special sequestration rules applied to federally funded health programs (medicare and veterans medical care), which could be cut by a maximum of only 2 percent under any sequestration. Automatic cost-of-living adjustments in the large entitlement programs, such as social security, were not subject to sequestration. Finally, interest outlays were completely outside the sequestration process.

As a result of these and other restrictions, OMB officials stated that approximately two-thirds of total outlays were "associated with budgetary resources exempt from sequestration. The burden of sequester falls on programs that comprise the remaining 34 percent . . . [of which] defense programs account for 46 percent, special rule nondefense programs account for 25 percent, and other nondefense programs account for 28 percent."[24] Although defense outlays accounted for only about one-fourth of total spending, defense programs would have to absorb roughly one-half of any sequester.[25]

The sequestration procedures under GRH II exposed almost the entire defense budget to automatic spending cuts, but the impact of that exposure obviously depended upon the magnitude of the cuts. For FY 1991, the magnitude was enormous, and the same economic factors that were expanding the FY 1991 deficit were creating outyear deficit-control problems that would inevitably lead to added defense sequesters.

It was readily apparent that a FY 1991 sequestration was not a realistic option. The challenge for both the Bush administration and Congress was constructing an alternative deficit-reduction plan. In the end, the administration was forced to make major concessions on tax policy and to scale down its defense planning, while Congress agreed to limits on discretionary domestic spending. The defense reductions remained firmly in place, despite the Persian Gulf crisis that erupted when Iraq invaded Kuwait on August 2. Much of the immediate cost of the *Desert Shield/Desert Storm* operation was covered by funds from foreign governments, and the rapid success with which the U.S. forces prosecuted the war with Iraq left essentially undisturbed the negotiated cutbacks in defense funding and force levels tied to the 1990 budget agreement.

The 1990 Budget Agreement

The budget summit that convened in the spring of 1990 took nearly 5 months to reach agreement. Sharp disagreements over tax policy, particularly capital gains taxation, and spending policy continually disrupted negotiations. Finally, on September 30, the White House announced that administration representatives and congressional negotiators had approved a 5-year, $500 billion deficit-reduction package.[26]

Despite bipartisan leadership support for the budget plan, members of both parties in the House of Representatives decisively rejected the compromise. A personal lobbying effort by President Bush failed to persuade House Republicans to support the budget plan's tax increases. Bush's nationwide appeal for public support also failed, triggering instead an unexpectedly negative response to the agreement and a decline in Bush's public support.[27] House Democrats, who objected to the plan's domestic spending limits, responded by deserting their leaders and joining with Republicans in a 179-254 defeat of the FY 1991 budget resolution on October 5.

Over the next 3 weeks, congressional Democrats rewrote major portions of the budget agreement. While the multiyear, $500 billion deficit-reduction targets contained in the initial agreement were retained, its tax policy provisions were significantly changed, as were its nondefense spending limits. In addition, Congress designed new budget enforcement procedures to protect deficit savings over the fiscal 1991-1995 period. The Omnibus Budget Reconciliation Act of 1990 (OBRA 1990), and the accompanying Budget Enforcement Act (BEA), were approved on October 27, nearly 4 weeks after the beginning of the new fiscal year. This broad and complex legislation revised the federal budget process and established a new framework for defense spending decisions.

The Omnibus Budget Reconciliation Act and Budget Enforcement Act of 1990

According to President Bush, the 1990 reconciliation package was the "centerpiece of the largest deficit reduction package in history."[28] The President also claimed that it included the "toughest enforcement system ever. The Gramm-Rudman-Hollings sequester process is extended and strengthened with caps, minisequesters, and a new 'pay-as-you-go' system."[29] The reconciliation bill of 1990, however, embodied a very different approach to deficit control than the GRH bills of 1985 and 1987, which had attempted to balance the budget through deficit ceilings and automatic spending cuts. The OBRA 1990 legislation controlled deficits indirectly by making it more difficult to increase spending or to reduce taxes.

The major components of this new approach to budget control included: (1) discretionary spending limits, or caps, for defense and nondefense programs; (2) pay-as-you-go requirements for legislation increasing entitlements or decreasing revenues; and (3) separate sequestration procedures to enforce the discretionary spending limits and the pay-as-you-go requirements.[30] Discretionary spending was separated from the remainder of the budget, in order to force cutbacks in either defense programs or nondefense programs, or in both. Entitlement spending, by comparison, was walled off in such a way as to restrict, but not eliminate, long-term growth rates.

Discretionary Spending. Approximately one-third of the nearly $500 billion in deficit-reduction savings under OBRA 1990 was allocated to discretionary spending (table 11). The discretionary spending savings, like the entitlement and revenue savings, were measured in terms of a baseline. (The baseline measurement shows the budgetary effect of a change in revenue or spending policy by comparing the revenue or spending level under existing law with the level under the changed law. For discretionary programs, the baseline represented the cost of existing policy adjusted for inflation.)

TABLE 11. *Allocation of deficit-reduction savings in the 1990 Omnibus Budget Reconciliation Act, fiscal years 1991-1995 (in billions of dollars)*

Policy Changes	Cumulative 5-Year Savings
Revenues	-$158
Entitlements and other mandatory spending	- 75
Discretionary spending*	- 190
Debt service savings	- 59
Total	-$482

*Includes enacted appropriations for FY 1991-1995 and required reductions in discretionary spending.

Source: *The Economic and Budget Outlook: Fiscal Years 1992-1996* (Washington, DC: Congressional Budget Office, 1991), xvii.

The annual appropriations limits on discretionary spending were below baseline levels. As estimated by the CBO, these appropriations limits produced outlay savings that rose from $13 billion in FY 1992 to $62 billion in FY 1995, compared to the baseline cost of discretionary programs. While the 1990 legislation allowed adjustments in the annual discretionary spending caps based upon, for example, unanticipated changes in inflation rates, the projected discretionary spending savings were reasonably firm. So long as the president and Congress complied with the appropriations limits, real discretionary spending would decline, and deficits would be reduced below baseline levels.

For the Bush administration, an important feature of the discretionary spending controls was a 3-year moratorium on defense-to-domestic transfers. For fiscal years 1991-1993, separate caps ("fire walls") were mandated for defense, international, and domestic programs (table 12). While Congress could, for example, appropriate less defense budget authority than the caps permitted, the savings could not be used to raise the caps for domestic or international programs. In fiscal years 1994 and 1995, the separate caps were merged, setting up direct competition among the discretionary spending categories. The aggregate limits for this latter period were also especially tight, thereby intensifying the competition.

The "fire walls" between defense and domestic appropriations offered the administration a temporary respite from congressional challenges to its defense budget program. During early 1990, for example, House Democrats had announced plans to reduce the defense budget well below Bush's request, and, on July 20, Armed Services Committee chairman Les Aspin had proposed an 8 percent cut in Bush's $307 billion FY 1991 defense authorization request. One week earlier, the Senate Armed Services Committee had approved a 6 percent reduction, to $289 billion, and the authorization measure faced the almost certain prospect of additional cuts on the Senate floor.

TABLE 12. *OBRA 1990 discretionary spending caps, fiscal years 1991-1995 (in billions of dollars)*

			Fiscal Year		
Category	1991	1992	1993	1994	1995
Defense					
Budget authority	$288.9	$291.6	$291.8	NA	NA
Outlays	297.7	295.7	292.7	NA	NA
International					
Budget authority	20.1	20.5	21.4	NA	NA
Outlays	18.6	19.1	19.6		
Domestic					
Budget authority	182.7	191.3	198.3	NA	NA
Outlays	198.1	210.1	221.7		
Total discretionary					
Budget authority	NA	NA	NA	510.8	517.7
Outlays	NA	NA	NA	534.8	540.8

Source: *Congressional Quarterly Almanac, 1990* (Washington, DC: Congressional Quarterly Inc., 1991), 161.

Iraq's invasion of Kuwait on August 2 affected the political climate on defense spending only marginally. On August 4, the Senate endorsed its Armed Services Committee's recommended defense cutbacks. Six weeks later, the House approved the slightly larger cuts reported out by its Armed Services Committee. In both chambers, additional reductions were rejected during floor debate, as were attempts to restore the higher funding levels requested by the Bush administration. The administration's strategic weapons program and conventional force structure proposals were endorsed by the Senate but challenged by the House. The House-passed defense authorization bill substantially altered both the administration's defense funding proposals and its defense planning priorities.

The 1990 budget agreement helped the Bush administration to turn back the House's challenge. The House-Senate conference, which started on October 2, ultimately accepted Defense Secretary Cheney's argument that Congress was obligated to support the $289 billion FY 1991 spending level contained in the budget pact. The conference approved, on October 17, a $288.3 billion defense authorization that sidestepped the more contentious policy issues that had divided the administration from Congress and the House from the Senate. The defense appropriations bill for FY 1991, which was signed by President Bush on November 5, embodied a similar approach. It affirmed the negotiated spending caps for FY 1991, while postponing major confrontations on weapons systems and force levels.

Entitlements and Other Mandatory Programs. The 1990 budget agreement did not establish dollar limits for nondiscretionary spending programs (entitlements and other direct spending).[31] Instead, the reconciliation bill made changes in existing entitlements that provided an estimated $75 billion in deficit savings for fiscal years 1991-1995. In addition, new budget enforcement rules governing entitlement spending were put into place.

The entitlement program savings enacted in 1990 primarily affected medicare and, to a lesser extent, farm price support programs. The medicare revisions included stricter limits on federal payments to healthcare providers, greater cost sharing for beneficiaries, and higher premiums for supplementary medical insurance (medicare Part B). The provider payment and cost-sharing provisions represented an estimated $35 billion in deficit-reduction savings through FY 1995.[32]

TABLE 13. *OBRA 1990 projected spending levels, fiscal years 1991-1995 (in billions of dollars)*

| | Fiscal Year | | | | |
Category	1991	1992	1993	1994	1995
Discretionary	$521	$526	$536	$536	$541
Defense	(299)	(295)	(292)		
Nondefense	(222)	(231)	(244)		
Entitlements	$632	$687	$731	$776	$824
Medicaid	(49)	(57)	(64)	(72)	(80)
Medicare	(114)	(127)	(140)	(156)	(173)
Social					
Security	(266)	(284)	(301)	(318)	(335)
All others	(203)	(219)	(226)	(230)	(236)
Deposit insurance	$103	$98	$48	$25	-$47
Net interest	$198	$207	$219	$227	$230

Source: *The Economic and Budget Outlook: Fiscal Years 1992-1996* (Washington, DC: Congressional Budget Office, 1991), 82, 91.

Projected growth rates for medicare and other large entitlements still remained high, particularly in comparison to discretionary spending (table 13). Over the 5-year period covered by the budget agreement, entitlement spending was expected to increase by nearly $200 billion, compared to $20 billion for total discretionary spending. Most of this entitlement growth was concentrated in three programs—medicaid (+$31 billion), medicare (+$59 billion), and social security (+$69 billion). Other entitlements were expected to grow slowly or, in a few instances, not at all.

Of particular relevance to spending control, the enforcement rules governing entitlements did not apply to actual spending levels. Medicare outlays, for example, could rise much more quickly than anticipated, so long as this occurred because of economic or other "uncontrollable" factors. The OBRA 1990 budget process only prohibited legislative changes in benefits, eligibility, or other statutory provisions that raised outlays for a given entitlement above the current policy baseline. The prohibition was not absolute, since an expansion in one entitlement could be financed through an offsetting cutback in another entitlement, an increase in revenues, or an increase in federal fees and other offsetting receipts. Without such offsets, however, new or expanded entitlements could not be enacted.

The pay-as-you-go system for entitlements, in other words, applied only to policy changes that would make the deficit higher than it otherwise would be. A similar approach was applied to revenue policy. In order to enact a tax cut, Congress would have to adopt an offsetting increase in another tax code provision or an offsetting reduction in an entitlement.[33]

Enforcement and Exemptions. The FY 1991-1995 discretionary spending caps and the entitlement and revenue policy controls were linked to separate enforcement provisions. The Budget Enforcement Act created a fairly straightforward sequestration procedure for discretionary spending. For fiscal years 1991-1993, discretionary spending above the statutory cap for any of the three spending categories would trigger an offsetting across-the-board spending cut for all nonexempt spending accounts within that category. For fiscal years 1994 and 1995, with an aggregate cap for discretionary spending, any across-the-board spending cut would be apportioned among all nonexempt discretionary spending accounts.

Sequestration for entitlement or revenue policy violations was to apply to nonexempt entitlement accounts, under a statutory formula that established a priority ranking for entitlements subject to sequestration. Any sequestration affecting medicare was limited, while social security was completely exempted from pay-as-you-go sequestration. The BEA removed the two main social security trust funds (the Old Age and Survivors Insurance trust fund and the Disability Insurance trust fund, or OASDI) from the unified budget, and established fire-wall protection procedures (in effect, separate pay-as-you-go controls) to insure that any increase in social security benefits or reduction in social security taxes would be offset by, respectively, a social security tax increase or a social security benefit cut.

Emergency spending waivers were also included in BEA for declarations of war or recessions. Funding for U.S. military operations in the Persian Gulf was designated as emergency spending, not subject to the defense spending cap. Contributions from other nations to defray the cost of Desert Shield were similarly excluded as offsets to discretionary spending. The defense spending limits were to become effective as soon as Operation *Desert Shield* ended.

Budget Tradeoffs

The 1990 budget policy and budget process changes incorporated a host of political compromises. The most conspicuous, and ultimately costly, compromise for President Bush was the breaking of his "no new taxes" pledge from the 1988 presidential campaign. Bush ultimately accepted an estimated $137 billion in new revenues for fiscal years 1991-1995, and the tax increases he agreed to were very different from those negotiated during the budget summit. Included among the post-budget summit tax changes initiated by congressional Democrats were a higher income tax structure and a personal exemption phaseout for upper-income taxpayers, along with a much higher wage base for the medicare payroll tax.[34] In another setback to his economic program, Bush failed to obtain more favorable tax treatment for small business incentive programs and for capital gains.[35]

The Bush administration also yielded to the Democrats on entitlement policy, since the pay-as-you-go system affected only new or expanded entitlements. The pay-as-you-go limitation was not an important concession on the part of congressional Democrats, since Bush's predecessor had been able to block entitlement expansions with no great difficulty.[36] What Reagan had been unable to do, of course, was to reverse existing entitlement policy and to reduce the budget share and GNP share devoted to entitlement spending. With the 1990 budget agreement, the Bush administration effectively foreclosed any effort to moderate the growth of existing entitlements, insuring that the budget share devoted to entitlement programs would continue to rise.

The administration's main goal during the budget summit was deficit control, but this goal was undermined in spite of the 1990 reconciliation act's substantial deficit savings and the multiyear discipline incorporated into the Budget Enforcement Act. Unfortunately, the economic downturn that started in 1990 turned out to be much more severe and prolonged than expected. As a result, revenues were depressed, entitlement spending increased sharply, and budget deficits quickly rose to unprecedented levels, making it impossible for the administration to claim credit for solving the deficit problem.

The Bush administration's secondary goal, to provide protection for its defense budget planning, was achieved, but only temporarily. In 1990 and 1991, the discretionary spending fire walls strengthened the administration's position during defense budget debates and served as an umbrella for effecting the transition from Cold War military budgets to the Bush administration's base force program. By 1992, however, the defense budget was once again the principal target of budget-cutting efforts.

The Base Force

The 1990 budget agreement and the defense authorization and appropriations bills for FY 1991 established general parameters for defense spending and force levels through the mid-1990s. During 1990, the Bush administration also began to elaborate a post-Cold War military strategy that would guide defense planning within these budgetary parameters. On August 2, 1990, in a speech at the Aspen Institute, President Bush had described the new strategic focus of U.S. policy, emphasizing the growing importance of major regional contingencies and the receding threat of Soviet-led aggression in Europe. According to Bush:

> Our task today is to shape our defense capabilities to these changing strategic circumstances. . . . [We] know that our forces can be smaller . . . [and] are hard at work determining the precise composition of the forces we need. But I can tell you now, we calculate that by 1995 our security needs can be met by an active force 25 percent smaller than today's. . . . What matters now is how we reshape the forces that remain.[37]

Over the next several months, Secretary of Defense Cheney and other defense officials spelled out the revised priorities for U.S. defense policy. Cheney identified four key elements: (1) strong offensive and defensive strategic capabilities, including robust research and development to support defenses against [weapons of mass destruction]; (2) forward deployments in "Asia, Europe, the Mediterranean, and the Atlantic, Pacific, and Indian Oceans . . . [with] forces sufficient to sustain those forward deployments and to reinforce them in the event of crisis"; (3) conventional forces for major regional contingencies and crisis response, including "the capability to deal with more than one concurrent regional contingency"; and (4) reconstitution capability for responding to a "major shift in Soviet strategy or the emergence of a major new threat."[38] Based upon these priorities and the 1990 budget agreement, the Bush administration developed a Future Years Defense Plan (FYDP) for fiscal years 1992-1997 that was formally submitted to Congress in early 1991.

This FYDP, and its accompanying budget submissions for fiscal years 1992 and 1993, incorporated both the reduced Soviet threat and the new defense budget limits into overall defense planning. Unlike prior FYDP's, which had often assumed unrealistically generous congressional appropriations, the FYDP for the fiscal year 1992-1997 period was deliberately based upon stringent defense budget levels.[39] These budget levels were linked to a considerably smaller military force structure designated as the base force.

Budget Strategy

The Bush administration's budget strategy for the base force had three central elements. First, the administration argued that Congress was obligated to appropriate up to, rather than below, the defense caps for fiscal years 1992 and 1993, an argument it hoped would be strengthened by the moratorium on transferring defense cuts to domestic programs. Second, since the base force could be funded within the defense spending limits for fiscal years 1992 and 1993, there was little incentive for Congress to attack the strategic rationale behind the base force program. With base force planning in place, it would then be more difficult for Congress to impose on defense the entire burden of complying with the tight discretionary spending caps in fiscal years 1994 and 1995. Third, if the base force could be protected through FY 1995, maintenance and modernization requirements would preclude significant future reductions and, indeed, might even necessitate modest real growth.[40]

This three-part strategy attempted to postpone defense policy confrontations with Congress as long as possible by depoliticizing defense spending totals. In 1991 and again in 1992, much of the administration's energy was directed toward preserving the discretionary spending fire walls rather than arguing the merits of the base force. The fire walls were preserved, but the administration's strategy was eventually overwhelmed by budgetary trends and political divisions it had tried to ignore.

The FY 1992 Budget. The defense appropriations request submitted by President Bush for FY 1992 was $290.8 billion, which was under the discretionary budget authority cap for defense.[41] (The incremental costs of Operation *Desert Shield/Desert Storm* were treated as off-budget and funding requirements were handled through supplemental appropriations.) As shown in table 14, the requested national defense funding levels for FY 1992, and the outyear projections, provided for approximately $175 billion in budget authority savings, and slightly less in outlay reductions, below 1991 baseline levels.

The largest component of the administration's scaled-back defense program was in military personnel costs. Active-duty personnel levels were to be reduced by about 320,000 over the fiscal year 1992-1995 period and the proposed cut in reserves was 270,000 over the same period. The recommended force structure changes, in units and overall manpower levels, are shown in table 15. The force structure changes also yielded major savings in other categories, such as operations and maintenance and procurement. While the administration's estimates of spending reductions from force level and force structure changes were considered to be fairly accurate, the savings it claimed in other areas were viewed as questionable. According to the General Accounting Office (GAO), the base force's unspecified management savings of approximately $70 billion (from a variety of initiatives in the administration's Defense Management Review) were unlikely to be realized in full, and its projected base closure savings of over $6 billion were grossly exaggerated (by perhaps $5.5 billion).[42]

Controversies about future costs had little impact on the FY 1992 defense budget debate. Congress passed its 1992 defense authorization and appropriations bills at the funding levels Bush had requested. Congress did cut back the administration's B-2 stealth bomber program while also limiting reserve personnel reductions, but there was no sustained effort either to impose deeper cuts on defense or to alter the basic structure of the defense program Bush had proposed.

This uncharacteristic congressional reticence during 1991 was not solely or even primarily a function of the budget agreement's fire walls. The U.S. military's remarkably successful performance in the Persian Gulf War had bolstered support of its leadership and personnel, while vindicating some controversial and expensive weapons systems. In contrast to the antidefense backlash after Vietnam, the response to the Persian Gulf War was overwhelmingly positive, greatly

61

TABLE 14. *Proposed major spending changes in the president's budget for function 050, national defense, fiscal years 1992-1996 (in billions of dollars)*

	FY 1992	FY 1993	FY 1994	FY 1995	FY 1996	Cumulative
		Baseline Budget Authority Reductions				
Military personnel	$ -4.6	$ -8.6	$ -16.5	$ -20.9	$ -23.8	$ -74.3
Operations and maintenance	-4.2	-10.2	-14.7	-18.3	-20.9	-68.3
Procurement	-5.9	-5.1	-5.8	-2.7	-5.5	-25.1
RDT&E	3.2	2.7	0.2	-4.0	-7.1	-5.0
Other	0.8	-2.2	0.9	-0.9	-1.6	-3.0
TOTAL	-16.9	-23.4	-35.9	-46.8	-58.8	-175.8
Bush FY 1992	$290.8	$290.9	$291.9	$295.1	$297.8	

<u>Baseline Outlay Reductions</u>

Military Personnel	-4.4	-8.3	-16.3	-20.6	-23.5	-73.2
Operations and maintenance	-3.8	-9.1	-13.5	-17.3	-20.1	-63.8
Procurement	-1.0	-2.9	-4.4	-4.1	-3.8	-16.2
RDT&E	1.5	2.4	1.2	-1.9	-5.1	-1.9
Other	0.8	-0.2	-1.2	-0.6	-0.9	-2.1
TOTAL	-6.9	-18.1	-34.2	-44.5	-53.5	157.2
Bush FY 1992	$298.2	$292.8	$290.4	$288.7	$289.6	

Source: *An Analysis of the President's Budgetary Proposals for Fiscal Year 1992* (Washington, DC: Congressional Budget Office, 1991), 63.

TABLE 15. *Changes in active forces and manpower, fiscal years 1990-1995*

	Fiscal Year		Decrease	
	1990	1995	Units	Percent
		Forces		
Army divisions				
Active	18	12	6	33
Reserve	10	6	4	40
Deployed aircraft carriers	13	12	1	8
Carrier air wings				
Active	13	11	2	15
Reserve	2	2	0	0
Battle force ships	545	451	94	17
Tactical fighter wings				
Active	24	15	9	38
Reserve	12	11	1	8
Strategic bombers	268	181	87	32
	Manpower (in thousands)			
Military				
Active	2,069	1,653	416	20
Reserve	1,128	906	222	20
Civilian	1,073	940	133	12

Source: *An Analysis of the President's Budgetary Proposals for Fiscal Year 1992* (Washington, DC: Congressional Budget Office, 1991), 69.

enhancing, at least for a time, the popularity and reputation of President Bush. Events during the latter part of 1991 that otherwise might have catalyzed aggressive peace dividend initiatives in Congress—ratification of the Conventional Forces in Europe treaty, completion of the Strategic Arms Reduction treaty negotiations, and the dissolution of the Soviet Union into independent republics—did not produce major defense cuts, although these events further strengthened the congressional opposition to strategic programs such as the B-2 bomber and the anti-missile defense program.

An additional ingredient in Congress' tentative handling of the defense budget was the deepening economic recession during 1991. With the deficit soaring, Congress was reluctant to exacerbate deficit-control problems, and, on three occasions, the Senate decisively voted against suspending the budget rules under the recession escape clause in the budget agreement. At the same time, members of Congress were concerned that stepped-up cuts in military personnel or procurement programs might worsen the recession.

In the absence of any budget agreement, the Bush administration probably would have been able to protect its defense program, at least during 1991. The budget agreement eased this task considerably, by eliminating protracted conflicts over spending policy. Congress approved its FY 1992 budget resolution on May 22, one of the earliest dates in nearly two decades, and then passed its major appropriations bills for FY 1992 in an equally prompt fashion.

The budget agreement had some less salutary, if unintended, effects. Because the defense spending bills for FY 1992 did not spark great controversy, the Bush administration did not find it necessary to mount a vigorous defense of its base force program. During the congressional debate over the FY 1992 defense budget, even administration supporters seemed reluctant to defend its defense spending requests on purely strategic grounds, relying instead on budget or economic policy arguments. Thus, the substantive case for the administration's defense program was never clearly articulated.

During much of 1991, and especially in the period

immediately following the Persian Gulf War, President Bush was at the height of his popularity, with public approval ratings that were exceptional for any president, and his political dominance of national security policy was probably as well-established as any president's since the end of World War II. It was therefore surprising that neither Bush nor other top administration officials capitalized upon this dominance to confront Congress directly on defense policy. The common assumption that Bush was unbeatable and would have a second term to mobilize support for a visionary defense strategy no doubt contributed to this caution, but the assumption was seriously mistaken.

The FY 1993 Budget. During 1992, budget policy battles between the administration and Congress became more heated, and discretionary spending served as the focal point for election-year maneuvering. The administration submitted a FY 1993 budget that pared both domestic and defense spending below the discretionary spending ceilings, and it threatened to veto any domestic appropriations bill that exceeded the president's budget. While Congress eventually conceded the battle on domestic spending, it gained a measure of revenge by forcing additional cuts in the administration's defense request.

President Bush's FY 1993 defense budget proposed rescinding, or canceling, nearly $8 billion in prior-year budget authority and recommended dropping current-year budget authority and outlay levels well under the BEA caps (table 16). The estimated savings under the FY 1993 defense program were approximately $50 billion for fiscal years 1993 to 1997, when compared to the defense budget submitted the previous year.[43] The administration claimed that these savings could be achieved without compromising the base force program's manpower levels or force structure, through cutting nearly $30 billion in procurement costs for the Seawolf submarine, B-2 bomber, and other weapons programs. In order to hold down ongoing weapons modernization costs, the administration proposed to direct funding toward research and development, rather than actual production and procurement, of new weapons systems.

TABLE 16. *Comparison of the administration's FY 1993 request for defense with the Budget Enforcement Act (BEA) caps for 1993 (in millions of dollars)*

Discretionary Budget Authority

BEA caps	$289,035
Administration's request	282,186
Difference	- 6,849

Discretionary Outlays

BEA caps	$296,824
Administration's request	293,462
Difference	- 3,362

Source: *An Analysis of the President's Budgetary Proposals for Fiscal Year 1993* (Washington, DC: Congressional Budget Office, 1992), 62.

These initiatives did not satisfy Congress. Neither the House nor the Senate supported efforts to remove the walls between defense and domestic discretionary spending, but the FY 1993 defense authorization and appropriations bills were reduced well below the President's budget and even further below the defense caps for FY 1993. In FY 1993, Congress appropriated $16 billion less for defense than it had in FY 1992, marking the first significant decline in current dollar spending since the 1970s.

Congress also rejected many of the procurement cutbacks in the administration's proposals, even though congressional funding levels were much more stringent. The FY 1993 appropriations bill for the Department of Defense targeted most of the spending cuts in operations and maintenance accounts (table 17). Because of its impact on combat readiness, operations and maintenance funding had been considered one of the safer elements in the Pentagon's budget, so the FY 1993 appropriations cuts did not portend well for future defense

TABLE 17. *Department of Defense appropriations, fiscal year 1993 (in millions of dollars)*

Category	Bush Request	House Bill	Senate Bill	Final Bill
Military personnel	$76,982.0	$76,896.2	$76,368.6	$76,275.0
Operations and maintenance	74,813.5	71,710.2	70,281.8	69,406.0
Procurement	55,610.0	53,743.3	52,103.2	55,375.9
Research and development	39,075.7	38,770.1	36,066.8	38,234.8
Revolving and management funds	1,123.8	16.6	2,325.2	1,737.2
Medical and other defense programs	12,616.9	11,278.4	11,172.8	11,027.8
Other agencies	199.6	168.9	213.4	246.6
Economic conversion	0	0	2,000.0	472.0
Miscellaneous provisions and scorekeeping adjustments	612.0	-717.0	153.8	1,011.3
Total	$261,133.5	$251,866.7	$250,685.6	$253,786.6

Source: *Congressional Quarterly Weekly Report* 50 (October 17, 1992): 3261.

funding. Congress' reluctance to force steep reductions in personnel and weapons procurement was bound to disappear once economic concerns eased. If operating costs were no longer to be accorded privileged status, the range of budget-cutting options would extend across the entire defense budget, with an additional downward impetus provided by the expiration of the discretionary spending fire walls after 1993.

Defense Strategy

The Bush election-year defense program proved to be politically weak, in part because national defense had been displaced by domestic economic problems but additionally because the strategic rationale for the base force had not been persuasively articulated to Congress or the public. The presidential campaign of 1992 did nothing to improve this situation. The Democratic party platform was carefully crafted to avoid the antidefense biases that had hurt the party in prior elections. In addition to setting out some general and noncontroversial priorities for defense planning, the platform also endorsed the decisive use of military force "when necessary to defend [U.S.] vital interests."[44] The Bush defense plan, it was charged, was simply "Cold War thinking on a smaller scale."[45] The platform, and the Clinton campaign, claimed that defense spending could be reduced by "comprehensive restructuring" without sacrificing defense capabilities.

The Republican platform was equally insipid, ignoring any serious discussion of defense strategy. The platform lauded the defense cuts that had already been made—elimination of over 100 weapons systems; closure or realignment of 550 overseas bases; reduction in military personnel of 25 percent; and additional spending reductions of nearly $35 billion over the next four years.[46] By 1997, the platform emphasized, defense would account for less than one-sixth of the budget, and its "proportion of gross domestic product, will be the lowest it has been since before World War II."[47]

What the Democrats would do, the platform warned, was to impose an additional $60 billion in cuts over 4 years, "throwing as many as 1 million additional Americans out of work," using the defense budget "as a bottomless piggy bank to try to beat swords into pork barrels," and reviving the "hollow military of the Carter era."[48]   The Bush campaign, like the Republican platform, never undertook a determined effort to explain the linkage between defense budgets and defense strategy.   The base force program was almost completely disregarded, which allowed the Clinton campaign to avoid any meaningful debate on defense policy.[49]

The Base Force and the Budget

From the beginning of the Bush presidency, congressional pressures to cut the defense budget were a constant threat in defense planning.   During its first year in office, the Bush administration sought to counter this threat by offering modest, and supposedly temporary, reductions in its defense program. Then, as the Cold War came to an end, the administration responded by establishing a strategic framework for the scope and pace of defense budget cuts.

The administration's effort to orchestrate the post-Cold War defense transition was ultimately unsuccessful, not because its base force program was implausible but rather because its approach to budget policy was flawed.   In exchange for what was. at best, marginal short-term protection for the defense budget, the Bush administration agreed to nondefense spending commitments that inevitably stripped away this protection.   By the end of the Bush presidency, federal spending policy had become even more skewed toward entitlements, while structural deficits had grown larger and more imposing.   George Bush's refusal to challenge Congress on spending policy doomed his battle for deficit control, and his reluctance to confront Congress on defense policy doomed his base force program as well.

Notes

1.   These pledges were included in the 1988 Republican platform, which also stated "It must be clear to all, except the leadership of the Democrat Party, that we are not beyond the era of threats to the security of the United States." *Congressional Quarterly Almanac,*

1988 (Washington, DC: Congressional Quarterly Inc., 1989), 74-A–75-A.

    2. *Congressional Quarterly Almanac, 1989* (Washington, DC: Congressional Quarterly Inc., 1990), 12-C.

    3. Ibid.

    4. Ibid., 85.

    5. Ibid.

    6. *The Economic and Budget Outlook: Fiscal Years 1993-1997* (Washington, DC: Congressional Budget Office, 1992), 103-04.

    7. Ibid.

    8. The sequestration rules for defense and domestic spending differed. About two-thirds of military spending was subject to sequestration, while more than two-thirds of domestic spending was exempt. About 15 percent of domestic spending was covered by special rules and limited reductions, with an additional 15 percent subject to full sequestration. For the total budget, only about one-fourth of spending was completely eligible for sequestration reductions, making large sequestrations extremely difficult, if not impossible. See Stanley E. Collender, *The Guide to the Federal Budget, Fiscal 1991* (Washington, DC: The Urban Institute, 1990), 77-80.

    9. *The Economic and Budget Outlook: Fiscal Years 1991-1995* (Washington, DC: Congressional Budget Office, 1990), 35-39.

    10. Ibid., 39.

    11. During his first year in office, Reagan is quoted as having stated, "I did not come here to balance the budget—not at the expense of my tax-cutting program and my defense program. If we can't do it in 1984, we'll have to do it later." Joseph White and Aaron Wildavsky, *The Deficit and the Public Interest* (Berkeley: University of California Press, 1989), 196. In 1981, Reagan repeatedly rejected the advice of his director of the Office of Management and Budget (OMB), David A. Stockman, to adjust his tax and defense programs in order to reduce the deficit. In 1989, Bush relied heavily upon his OMB director, Richard G. Darman, to negotiate a budget policy agreement with Congress. The long confirmation battle over John G. Tower's nomination as Bush's first Secretary of Defense made it much more difficult for the Department of Defense to oppose Darman's defense cuts. The Senate finally rejected the Tower nomination on March 9. Bush's second nominee, House minority whip Richard B. Cheney, was confirmed on March 17, by which time cuts from the Reagan defense program had already been announced. Three days

before his confirmation, Cheney assured members of the Senate Armed Services Committee that he would work to implement the planned reductions. *Congressional Quarterly Almanac, 1989*, 411.

12. *Budget of the United States Government, Fiscal Year 1991* (Washington, DC: GPO, 1990), 152.

13. Ibid.

14. *Congressional Quarterly Almanac, 1990* (Washington, DC: Congressional Quarterly Inc., 1991), 672.

15. Congress, House, Committee on Armed Services, *The Fading Threat: Soviet Conventional Military Power in Decline* (Washington, DC: GPO, 1990), 195-98.

16. Ibid., 1. This was the view of the Democratic members of the Defense Policy Panel on the Armed Services Committee.

17. Ibid., 12.

18. Ibid., 18.

19. Ibid., 223.

20. Ibid., 15-16.

21. *Budget of the United States Government, Fiscal Year 1991*, 9.

22. Ibid., 11.

23. *National Journal* 22 (May 19, 1990): 1240.

24. *Budget of the United States Government, Fiscal Year 1991*, A-35.

25. The president had authority to shelter military personnel accounts from sequester, but doing so would have reduced sequestrable defense accounts to 40 percent of overall defense outlays and to less than 10 percent of total budget outlays. In 1989, when a partial sequester was implemented, the Bush administration did not exercise the personnel exemption precisely in order to avoid such a disproportionate reduction in nonpersonnel accounts. Its subsequent request for greater flexibility in implementing the defense sequester was blocked by congressional Democrats, forcing the administration to get congressional approval for reprogramming funds to cover shortfalls in personnel accounts. *Congressional Quarterly Almanac, 1990*, 676.

26. The White House representatives were chief of staff John H. Sununu, OMB Director Richard G. Darman, and Secretary of the Treasury Nicholas F. Brady. The House and Senate negotiators included party and committee leaders, with the latter drawn from the Appropriations, Budget, Ways and Means, and Finance committees.

27. See Daniel Franklin, *Making Ends Meet: Congressional Budgeting in the Age of Deficits* (Washington, DC: Congressional Quarterly Press, 1993), 79.

28. *Congressional Quarterly Almanac, 1990,* 166.

29. Title XIII of the Omnibus Budget Reconciliation Act of 1990 (PL 101-508) contained the enforcement provisions that were to be applied to discretionary spending, entitlements and mandatory spending, and revenues. Title XIII was designated as the Budget Enforcement Act (BEA).

30. There was, in addition, an aggregate sequestration procedure linked to maximum deficit amounts. It was unlikely that this procedure would be used in fiscal years 1991-1993, since it essentially applied to legislated excess spending already covered by the separate sequestration procedures for discretionary spending and pay-as-you-go programs. For fiscal years 1994 and 1995, maximum deficit targets could be adjusted, making an aggregate sequestration highly unlikely.

31. The pay-as-you-go requirement formally applied to direct spending, which was defined as spending for entitlements, for food stamps, and for any other programs not subject to appropriations controls.

32. *Congressional Quarterly Almanac, 1990,* 143-46.

33. While federal government deposit insurance is a mandatory spending program, it was exempted from the pay-as-you-go rules. See *The Economic and Budget Outlook: Fiscal Years 1992-1996* (Washington, DC: Congressional Budget Office, 1991), 94.

34. Ibid., 92-93.

35. Ibid., 91.

36. See Dennis S. Ippolito, *Uncertain Legacies, Federal Budget Policy from Roosevelt through Reagan* (Charlottesville: University Press of Virginia, 1990), 181-90.

37. *Report of the Secretary of Defense to the President and the Congress, January 1991* (Washington, DC: GPO, 1991), 131.

38. Ibid., 4-5.

39. See *Testimony, Defense Budget and Program Issues Facing the 102nd Congress* (Washington, DC: Government Accounting Office, 1991), 5.

40. *Staff Memorandum, Fiscal Implications of the Administration's Proposed Base Force* (Washington, DC: Congressional Budget Office, 1991), 11-15.

41. See *An Analysis of the President's Budgetary Proposals for Fiscal Year 1992* (Washington, DC: Congressional Budget Office, 1991), 62-66.

42. *Testimony, Defense Budget and Program Issues*, 5-7.

43. See *An Analysis of the President's Budgetary Proposals*, 61-65.

44. *Congressional Quarterly Weekly Report* 50 (July 18, 1992): 2111.

45. Ibid.

46. *Congressional Quarterly Weekly Report* 50 (August 22, 1992): 2580.

47. Ibid.

48. Ibid.

49. The Republican platform did, however, attempt to inject the "family values" issue into the defense debate.

3. Post-Cold War Transition II: The Clinton Program

DURING THE 1992 PRESIDENTIAL campaign, defense policy never emerged as a highly salient issue. A deep economic recession in the United States, coupled with the collapse of the Soviet threat, concentrated the electorate's attention on domestic economic policy. In addition, the third-party candidacy of H. Ross Perot altered the dynamics of the campaign, blurring traditional divisions on defense issues and subordinating the debate over the defense budget to deficit reduction.

With economic recovery and deficit control overshadowing national security policy, each of the three leading candidates for president recommended sizable defense budget cuts. In mid-October of 1992, George Bush proposed an additional $25 billion in multiyear reductions from his own defense budget program.[1] Bill Clinton's economic and budget plan called for approximately $60 billion in defense cuts over 4 years from the FY 1993 Bush defense program, while Perot's plan specified $40 billion less over 5 years.[2] The defense budget was targeted as well for extensive cutbacks in nearly all of the highly publicized deficit-reduction programs being circulated by congressional leaders and public policy organizations.[3]

The 1992 election marked a conspicuous departure from the preceding several presidential races, each of which had featured meaningful partisan and ideological differences over defense policy.[4] The 1992 race was unusual in that the differences over defense spending were argued in terms of defense's contribution to deficit reduction, and the lack of any serious discussion of defense policy virtually guaranteed that defense cuts would expand after the election, regardless of who won. Further, with neither Clinton nor Bush willing to promote major entitlement cutbacks, a growing deficit-reduction burden would fall on discretionary spending and, inevitably, on defense.

Bill Clinton's victory accentuated this inevitability, since his economic program called for discretionary domestic spending increases. Moreover, with Clinton's having sidestepped any clearly defined defense program, defense budgets would be even more exposed to congressional attacks. Clinton's victory over Bush meant that Congress would be cutting from lower presidential defense budgets, without the "base force" or a settled alternative providing protection against further cuts, and with an administration sharing its commitment to satisfy domestic transfer pressures.

The political pressures to cut defense were stronger in the aftermath of the 1992 presidential election than they had been in quite some time. It was evident, as Bill Clinton took office, that defense would be substantially reduced over the short term, because of other budget priorities. More important, the downward trend for defense would almost certainly continue, since domestic spending commitments and structural deficits would become even more entrenched.

The Budget Policy Context

Economic forecasts during 1992 confirmed that policymakers faced an unrelenting deficit-control problem. In August, the CBO reported that the deficit would "settle into a stubborn, long-run level of nearly 4 percent of gross domestic product (GDP) even after the temporary effects of the recession and high deposit insurance wane."[5] According to the CBO, budget deficits might average nearly $240 billion annually through the late 1990s, excluding emergency spending and controlling for cyclical economic factors.[6] Unless current policy was radically altered, deficits would start to increase in the late 1990s, reaching the $500 billion mark in 2002.[7]

Discretionary Spending

The CBO's projections, which were tacitly accepted by the Bush administration, stressed that deficits would not decline, much less disappear, even if tight discretionary spending caps were extended indefinitely. Over the long term, deficits would grow regardless of discretionary spending controls, because entitlement spending increases would overwhelm discretionary savings. For defense, the dimension and persistence of the deficit-control quandary made it unlikely that budgetary pressures would eventually diminish.

Complicating the budgetary squeeze on defense was the immediate problem of the discretionary spending caps, which required real cuts in total discretionary spending during fiscal years 1994 and 1995. Whatever assumptions the Bush administration's budget summit negotiators had made in 1990 about how this reduction might be equitably apportioned between defense and domestic programs, any prospects for cuts in discretionary domestic programs had disappeared 2 years later. Under the discretionary caps for fiscal years 1994 and 1995, maintaining domestic programs at baseline levels would require $20 to $30 billion in defense reductions from FY 1993.[8]

For defense supporters in Congress, domestic transfer pressures were rapidly building. When the Senate Armed Services Committee held its defense planning hearings early in 1992, it was inundated with proposals for immediately expanding defense budget reductions. The congressionally-sponsored plans called for $100 to $200 billion in multiyear defense cuts, prompting Armed Services Committee chairman Sam Nunn, to complain that "some of them are based on how much they have in mind for other spending, or for tax cuts. . . . Our job is . . . a threat-based analysis, and that is a totally different thing than picking out your favorite spending program and saying this is how much we ought to cut defense."[9]

Comprehensive Budget Control

The defense budget's political support and budgetary exposure were moving in opposite directions during 1992, making it difficult to check mounting demands for defense cuts. What was needed in order to relieve the pressure on defense was a concerted attack on entitlement spending, but Nunn admitted that no one was willing to confront entitlements:

77

What is most discouraging to me, I say, is that people do look at the defense budget as being able to solve our budget problems. If you look at the growth . . . the growth has been in entitlement programs. That is what is squeezing the discretionary spending. That is what is squeezing everything and this is what is causing a huge amount of our deficit.

But nobody talks about entitlement programs. They have been labelled the sacred cow and so people do not talk about them; and that is both political parties. That is both the executive branch and the Congress. . . . So we are becoming more and more on automatic pilot and the automatic pilot is huge, huge deficits.[10]

The major party platforms in 1992 confirmed Nunn's indictment. The Republican platform promised that "A Republican Congress, working with a Republican President, will consider non-Social Security mandatory spending portions of the budget when looking for savings."[11] The Democratic platform pledged to "tackle spending by putting everything on the table," but mentioned only "soaring health-care costs" as a possible entitlement reform.[12]

The economic plans issued by the Bush and Clinton campaigns did not go much further. Bush's deficit-control proposals included a cap on entitlement spending that his advisers claimed would save nearly $300 billion over 5 years.[13] While an entitlement cap had been mentioned in the Bush administration's budgets, few program cuts had been specified, so it was impossible to assess how $300 billion in savings might be achieved. Moreover, since the administration had never seriously pushed for its entitlement cap proposal, the commitment to any future entitlement reform was questionable as well as vague.

The economic recovery plan put forth by Bill Clinton likewise included few specifics on entitlements. The Clinton plan proposed raising medicare insurance premiums, but this provided less than $5 billion in estimated savings over 4 years.[14] Healthcare savings, which were an important part of Clinton's deficit-reduction program, were not identified during the campaign.

Unlike the two major party candidates, Ross Perot propounded specific cutbacks in entitlement programs. Perot's proposals included reductions in farm subsidies and in cost-of-living-adjustments (COLAs) for federal retirees, increases in medicare premiums, and higher taxation of social security benefits. When combined with large but imprecise "cost containment" reductions in medicare and medicaid, Perot's entitlement policy savings were projected at nearly $270 billion in 5-year savings.[15] Perhaps most noteworthy, Perot was the only leading candidate to raise the prospect of means-testing entitlements, although he quickly dropped the idea as politically untenable.

Perot's off-and-on candidacy compounded his difficulties in developing support for entitlement reforms. After Perot reentered the race on October 1, he attempted to revive the deficit-control issue but was unable to force Bush or Clinton to join any consequential debate on comprehensive spending control. As a result, deficit reduction retained its customary vagueness, allowing entitlement spending to be ignored.

The budget policy context defining defense spending options became even more unfavorable during 1992. Even as the long-term deficit outlook worsened, it proved impossible to attack the root cause of deficits. With discretionary spending supplying substantial, if inadequate, budgetary restraint, defense and nondefense programs were competing for diminishing resources. If George Bush had won the election, it was decidedly improbable that his $1.43 trillion fiscal 1993-1997 defense spending plan could survive this competition intact. Clinton's victory enhanced the prospects for even greater defense transfers to domestic programs.

Once in office, the Clinton administration quickly recognized that defense cuts had to be expedited in order to accommodate domestic spending initiatives. The administration also expanded multiyear defense savings in order to achieve its deficit-reduction goals. This budget-driven approach instantly eliminated the base force as a defense policy option. The responsibility for developing an alternative defense program was assumed by Secretary of Defense Aspin, who had been

Congress' most prominent base force critic during his tenure as chairman of the House Armed Services Committee.

The "Two Revolutions" and the Base Force

The Bush administration's base force program had been unveiled during the latter part of 1990, after the first Soviet "revolution" removed the Warsaw Pact as a political entity and military threat. One year later, a second Soviet revolution unfolded, beginning with the failed coup of August 19, 1991, and ending 4 months later with the dissolution of the Soviet Union and creation of the Commonwealth of Independent States. Given this chronology, the administration's detractors in Congress charged that the base force concept, and its underlying budgetary requirements, disregarded the greatly diminished threat ensuing from the second revolution.

Revolution One

Despite congressional complaints that the base force was too expensive, initial efforts to pare the Bush administration's defense program were stymied first by the Persian Gulf crisis and almost immediately thereafter by upheavals in the Soviet Union. Early in 1991, Soviet troops used force against independence movements in the Baltic States, prompting Congress to adopt a concurrent resolution condemning the Soviet Union and calling upon President Bush to coordinate allied sanctions against the Soviet Union if the violence continued. A U.S.-Soviet summit, originally scheduled for mid-February 1991, was postponed, with both the administration and Congress expressing skepticism about the pace and direction of change under Gorbachev. By the end of July, however, tensions began to ease. The Strategic Arms Reduction Treaty (START) was concluded and signed, after 9 years of negotiations. Plans were announced for a jointly-sponsored U.S.-Soviet Middle East peace conference, and the Bush administration completed a U.S.-Soviet trade agreement for submission to Congress.[16]

Several weeks later, a coup was launched against

Gorbachev's government. The coup quickly collapsed, but in its wake the Soviet republics declared their independence, forcing Gorbachev to resign and to yield power to Russian President Boris Yeltsin. This sudden and unanticipated turbulence left the administration and Congress groping for an appropriate policy response.

The "climate of uncertainty" in the former Soviet Union was seized upon by the Bush administration to argue against cutbacks in its defense program, even modest efforts to divert defense funds to assist the Soviet republics. On August 28, 1991, House Armed Services Committee chairman Aspin proposed taking $1 billion from the defense budget and creating a "Humanitarian Aid and Stabilization Fund" to provide assistance to the Soviet Union. Aspin warned that the United States should not allow "the first winter of freedom after 70 years of communism to be a disaster for the Soviet Union."[17] In justifying the defense transfer, Aspin claimed, "This is defense by different means, but defense nevertheless, so it should come out of the Pentagon budget."[18]

The Bush administration's first response to Aspin's initiative was extremely negative. The President declared, "I think it's way too premature. I'm not going to go out there and say we can afford to cut defense."[19] Defense Secretary Cheney also opposed any defense reduction, warning, "Five years from now, who will control the Soviet nuclear arsenal? Will there still be a central government in charge?"[20] Although Senate Armed Services Committee chairman Sam Nunn supported Aspin's attempt to include the Soviet aid provision in the fiscal 1992 defense authorization bill, many of their fellow Democrats contended that monies diverted from defense should be used to help the domestic economy and to aid U.S. workers. The Bush administration eventually backed off its charge that Aspin's proposal violated the budget agreement's rules against discretionary spending transfers, but it refused to lend active support to the aid plan. Lacking administration backing, Aspin and Nunn were forced to withdraw their proposal.

Revolution Two

Several weeks later, Congress adopted a $500 million assistance package that included funds for helping dismantle Soviet nuclear weapons and for transporting humanitarian assistance. Once again, the administration was on the sidelines, but on this occasion congressional Republicans helped to pass the required authorization and appropriations measures just before Congress adjourned. After the legislation was signed by President Bush on December 12, Secretary of State James Baker announced plans to draw immediately upon the new funding, warning that "time for action is short. Much as we will benefit if this revolution succeeds, we will pay if it fails."[21] Baker then pledged to seek additional funds for technical assistance to the Soviet economy and invited world leaders to a Washington conference to coordinate various aid programs.

Aspin welcomed the Baker initiatives, calling them "a qualitative step forward."[22] Aspin also stated, "Until this announcement, the administration's response to the opportunities and dangers of the post-coup former Soviet Union has been tepid and piecemeal."[23] Less than 2 weeks after Baker's announcements, the Soviet Union had been dissolved.

This second revolution further weakened the already shaky congressional support for the base force and its corollary funding needs. Most base force critics were willing to concede that the 25 percent force reduction initiated by the Bush administration was a reasonable response to the elimination of the Warsaw Pact threat to Western Europe.[24] These critics were unwilling to grant the same concession once the Soviet threat had diminished. According to Aspin, "[T]he base force . . . was a proposal on defense spending which was put forward in August of 1990," more than 1 year before the "Soviet Union came off the table."[25]

> I would contend that . . . [the] base force takes into account the first revolution but not the second revolution, and that what we need to do now in the light of the two revolutions is a bottom-up review of what we have to do with defense. . . . The point to make

here is that what we are doing is different from where [Secretary of Defense] Cheney is. It is essentially a difference of perspective. His was as of August of 1990; ours is as of January of 1992. There have been a lot of things happen in that 18-month period in between.[26]

The Bush administration's defense spokesmen rejected the Aspin critique as misleading. In hearings before the Senate Armed Services Committee held early in 1992, General Colin Powell declared that the base force concept did not represent top-down force restructuring, nor did it ignore "the revolutions that have taken place in the Soviet Union over the last couple of years."[27]

We began planning the Base Force and our new National Military Strategy over 2 years ago. It was not based on the situation that existed 2 years ago. It was based on what we could reasonably see happening in the years ahead. And frankly, we were quite prophetic and prescient. . . . We anticipated much of what has happened.

The Base Force was not a force locked in concrete 2 years ago for a situation that existed 2 years ago. It was a force designed for how we anticipated the world would move. . . . I think we did a pretty good job of anticipating that [second revolution]. But what nobody can anticipate is the third revolution or the fourth revolution or the fifth revolution.[28]

The administration could hardly deny, however, that funding for the base force would necessarily come at the expense of domestic programs.

Among congressional Democrats, there was extensive support for cutting defense well below base force requirements and diverting the funds to domestic programs, but this approach carried with it the possibility of tainting the party's presidential nominee with the "anti-defense reputation" that had plagued previous Democratic candidates. Aspin, who was especially concerned about this problem, believed that the solution was a Democratic party defense policy that would serve as "a 'cocoon' for the nominee—a protective covering and responsible coloration on defense."[29] Further, this Democratic defense program would supply the defense budget savings needed to accommodate a Democratic domestic agenda.

Defense Spending and Force Options

The gestation of what would eventually become the Clinton campaign's "defense program" began with the FY 1993 budget cycle in the House. On February 26, 1992, Armed Services Committee chairman Aspin appeared before the House Budget Committee to recommend a $12-$15 billion budget authority reduction in the FY 1993 defense budget request submitted by the Bush administration.[30] Aspin stated that "[r]eductions of more than $15 billion for whatever purpose would represent too steep a decline in military capability."[31] While acknowledging the possibility of extending and expanding FY 1993 savings in future years, Aspin cautioned against doing so before decisions on an underlying force structure had been determined.

The House Role on Defense

The groundwork for Aspin's recommendations to the Budget Committee had been established the previous fall, when House Speaker Thomas S. Foley convened a meeting of Democratic defense and budget committee leaders to review defense planning alternatives.[32] Aspin was assigned the primary responsibility for identifying military force options and corresponding defense funding requirements to structure upcoming defense debates. An important goal of Foley's planning effort was to strengthen the House's influence on defense policy matters, particularly in bargaining with the Senate.

Prior to the Persian Gulf War, the Senate Armed Services Committee and its chairman, Sam Nunn, had consistently overshadowed their House counterparts. Dealing with a less fractious committee and a less sharply divided chamber than Aspin faced, Nunn had been able to orchestrate a coherent Senate position on most important defense matters. Nunn had also succeeded in moderating demands for large defense cuts during Senate floor debates and during conference committee deliberations with the House.

The Persian Gulf War cast Aspin and the House into new-found prominence. Aspin's forceful, public support of the congressional resolution authorizing President Bush to go to war with Iraq contrasted sharply with Nunn's opposition. The House Armed Services Committee's hearings and reports on military options against Iraq also strengthened the case for the use of force, again in contrast to the more cautious and tentative hearings record produced in the Senate. Finally, the 250-183 House vote in favor of the use of force resolution demonstrated unexpected cohesion among moderate Democrats on an intensely divisive vote. Indeed, some Democrats feared that what the leadership had designated as a "conscience vote" would lead to a lasting rift within the party. Instead, the rapid success of Operation *Desert Storm* quickly healed the rift and strengthened the influence of interventionist Democrats in defense policy debates.

Nevertheless, many House Democrats remained strongly committed to massive defense cuts, making it doubtful that any post-Gulf War caution in pressing their claims would last for very long. With the subsequent collapse of the Soviet Union setting the stage for a full-scale assault on defense spending levels, the House faced the likelihood of extreme politicization on budget policy. For Aspin and like-minded Democrats, the challenge was to develop a party consensus on defense that would balance the strong budgetary pressures working against defense with politically credible national security requirements.

The Aspin Plan's Force Equivalents

The approach utilized by Aspin and his Armed Services Committee staff was threat-based force planning to generate force options and corresponding budgetary requirements. The Aspin plan identified six situations or purposes for which military force might be required, while designating regional aggressors as the "main threat driver" (see table 18). The gross size of the U.S. force structure was defined primarily in terms of regional threats, with "force shaping" decisions (equipment, personnel expertise and training, research and development, etc.) rather than size requirements being the dominant consideration for the remaining military purposes.

TABLE 18. *Situations for which military forces might be required, 1992 Aspin Plan*

Countering Regional Aggressors (Middle East and Southwest Asia; North Korea; and Elsewhere)

Combatting the Spread of Nuclear and Other Mass Terror Weapons (Rogue Regional Powers and Others)

Fighting Terrorism (State Sponsors and Terrorist Groups)

Restricting Drug Trafficking

Peacekeeping Operations

Humanitarian Assistance Operations

Source: Congress, House, Committee on Armed Services, Representative Les Aspin, *An Approach to Sizing American Conventional Forces for the Post-Soviet Era,* February 25, 1992, 6.

The Foundation Block. The threat-based contingency planning proposed by Aspin assumed maintenance of an adequate defense foundation. Included in this foundation were strategic nuclear forces, along with special operations forces, defense forces for U.S. territory, and overseas forces providing a U.S. presence. In order to support these and other forces, appropriate levels of investment (research and development and procurement for force modernization) and readiness (training and operating tempos necessary to sustain high levels of readiness) would have to be supported. In addition, the necessary industrial base would have to be available.

Each of these foundation blocks was discussed briefly in the Aspin plan, but specifics about size and cost were not included.

In particular, the "forces for overseas presence" were unspecified. The quantitative focus of the Aspin plan, however, was not on defense foundation requirements but rather on the potential threat requirements, among which regional threats were the dominant concern.

The Iraq Equivalent. The quantitative dimension of the regional threat focus utilized an "Iraq Equivalent," with pre-Gulf War Iraq serving as the "very model of a modern, post-Soviet regional" threat.[33] Conceding that "No future conflict will be exactly the same as the war with Iraq, nor will any future adversary exactly match Iraq's circumstances," Aspin argued that Iraq's offensive power prior to the Gulf War was a valid "generic threat measure."[34] Aspin then proffered the *Desert Storm* Equivalent as a valid measure of the U.S. forces required to deal with an Iraq Equivalent threat.[35]

The Desert Storm *Equivalent.* The potential regional threats identified by Aspin included post-war Iraq, Iran, Syria, and Libya, along with North Korea, China, and Cuba. The land, sea, and air forces for each of these countries were measured in terms of Iraq Equivalents, although the land forces ("specifically the heavy mechanized and armored forces") were singled out as representing the "bulk of an offensive capability required to commit regional aggression."[36] Air forces and navies were, in each instance, judged to be markedly inferior in size and capabilities, thereby posing no serious obstacle to U.S. forces.

Aspin's regional threat analysis concluded that pre-war Iraq constituted a more substantial military threat than any of the other countries the U.S. might possibly be required to engage.[37] Thus, the U.S. forces necessary to meet these potential threats could realistically be gauged in terms of the Persian Gulf conflict, but rather than using the forces actually deployed, the *Desert Storm* Equivalent was defined as a "conservatively estimated force that mattered in defeating Saddam Hussein and that also could have defeated him under somewhat different scenarios."[38] The overall force structure options geared to regional threats included the "basic force that mattered," along with augmented offensive and defensive capabilities that either could have countered an early Iraqi attack on Saudi Arabia or could have allowed U.S. forces to delay indefinitely an offensive against Iraq (table 19).

TABLE 19. *The* Desert Storm *equivalent force measure, basic and augmented*

Basic "Force that Mattered"
   Six heavy divisions
   One light division (air-transportable, early-arriving)
   One land Marine division
   One+ Marine brigades at sea
   24 Air Force fighter squadrons
   70 heavy bombers
   Four carrier battle groups (two early-arriving; Aegis defenses; cruise missile launch capability)

Possible Augmentations
   Additional fast sealift and/or afloat pre-positioning of equipment
   Additional rotation capability

Source: Congress, House, Committee on Armed Services, Representative Les Aspin, *An Approach to Sizing American Conventional Forces for the Post-Soviet Era,* February 25, 1992, 15.

Additional Equivalents. With the *Desert Storm* Equivalent defining the desired force structure for responding to a major regional aggression, other recent U.S. military actions in Central America and the Middle East were used to appraise smaller capabilities. Operation *Just Cause* in Panama served as a loose surrogate for the comparatively small forces that might be needed to fight terrorism, restrict drug trafficking, or combat the spread of mass terror weapons. The remaining capability for which U.S. forces might be required, peacekeeping operations and humanitarian assistance, was measured in terms of a *Provide Comfort* Equivalent. This last equivalent comprised the forces used to provide assistance to the Kurds after the Persian Gulf War, along with the relief effort mounted during the *Sea Angel* Operation.

Applying the Equivalents

The three building blocks of capability—the *Desert Storm* Equivalent, the Panama Equivalent, and the *Provide Comfort* Equivalent—provided measures of force size but not a defined force structure. In assessing force structure options, the Aspin plan discussed the implications of multiple contingencies, varying durations for the commitment of forces, and varying requirements for delivering forces. Each of the force structure options in the Aspin plan assumed multiple contingencies and incorporated lift and prepositioning capabilities described as superior to those projected in the base force plan. The options differed in the number and type of multiple contingencies and in the rotation base necessary to support forward deployed troops.

The resulting array of force structure options is shown in figure 2. The smallest, Force A, envisioned one Iraq-sized regional contingency and a humanitarian assistance operation comparable to *Provide Comfort.* Despite Force A's small size, Aspin claimed, "it would be able to project combat power more quickly than the Administration's much larger Base Force for the one regional contingency because of the additional sealift and afloat prepositioning provided."[39]

Force B added a simultaneous capability for a second regional contingency (Korea, Europe, or elsewhere) in which a *Desert Storm* Equivalent of U.S. air strike power would support major ground forces provided by U.S. allies. Force B also included supplementary fast sealift and afloat prepositioning for rapid deployment of U.S. forces. In Force C, added options included an augmented rotation base that could sustain a *Desert Storm*-sized deployment for an extended period and a Panama-sized contingency force to handle a simultaneous third conflict. Force D provided additional forces "for a more robust response to all three simultaneous contingencies. . . . [and] a second humanitarian aid operation the size of Provide Comfort at the same time."[40]

FIGURE 2. *Contingencies and force structure options*

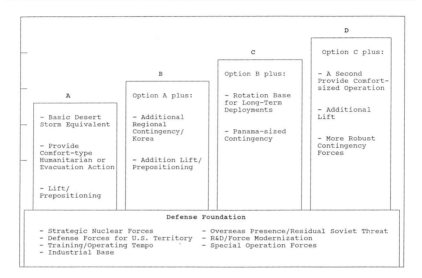

Source: Congress, House, Committee on Armed Services, Representative Les Aspin, *An Approach to Sizing American Conventional Forces for the Post-Soviet Era,* February 25, 1992, chart II.

The Base Force and Option C

While presenting several options for force planning, Aspin expressed to the House Budget Committee "a preliminary preference for providing the military with capabilities comparable to those in Option C . . . [although] the final decision on a force option will have to wait until the Committee on Armed Services can hold hearings this spring [of 1992]."[41] Aspin also stated, "If political and military developments worldwide move further in our favor, it may be possible to make cuts that go deeper than Option C in fiscal year 1994 and beyond."[42]

The attractiveness of the Force C option, for Aspin and others, lay in its distinctive balancing of military and budgetary needs. Each of Aspin's options called for a smaller-sized force than the Bush administration's base force program, but their projected personnel reductions and budgetary savings differed significantly. By fiscal year 1997, the base force projected active-duty personnel reductions of approximately 350,000 below the fiscal year 1991 end force level (see Table 3.3). The Force A and Force B options entailed additional cuts of between 300,000 and 400,000 active-duty personnel, while Force C limited these reductions to about 200,000. Projected Force D active duty personnel levels, by contrast, were close to base force levels.

The configuration of forces under Force D was quite different from the base force, as indeed were the force structures for each of the remaining Aspin plan options (table 21). Force levels for the Army and Air Force were considerably lower than the base force under all of the alternative defense options, while sealift requirements were higher. The Navy would shrink well below base force levelsunder Force Options A, B, and C, but Force D would add two carriers and 32 assault ships to the base force naval plan, while cutting total ships by less than 5 percent.

Described as smaller but superior to the base force in providing "much more early arriving military capability on a more self-reliant basis anywhere in the world, to cope with the greater diversity in contingencies . . . in the more fluid post-Soviet world," Force D was also slightly more costly than the base force and other force options.[43] Measured against the FY 1992 baseline, Force D would provide only $15 billion in budget authority cuts over five years (table 22). The most recent base force proposal,ich the Bush administration had submitted to Congress in its FY 1993 budget, yielded projected savings nearly triple those under Force D. Since it was inconceivable that Congress would support higher defense spending than the Bush administration had recommended, Force D was not a realistic option, regardless of its substantive merits. Force A and Force B provided four to five times the budget reductions of the Bush program but achieved these savings by sacrificing important military capabilities. In the context of a presidential election year, Force A and Force B would probably prove troublesome for a Democratic party that had suffered in the past from an antidefense reputation.

TABLE 20. *Force structure and force level comparisons, fiscal year 1991 end force and fiscal year 1997 alternative forces*

	FY 1991 End Force	FY 1997 Base Force	FY 1997 Force A	FY 1997 Force B	FY 1997 Force C	FY 1997 Force D
ARMY						
Active divisions	16	12	8	8	9	10
Reserve divisions	10	6	2	2	6	6
Cadre Divisions	0	2	0	0	0	0
MARINE CORPS						
Active divisions	3	2.33	2	2	2	3
Reserve divisions	1	1	1	1	1	1
AIR FORCE						
Active wings	22	15	6	8	10	11
Reserve wings	12	11	4	6	8	9

NAVY

Ships (total)	528	450	220	290	340	430
Carriers	15	13	6	8	12	15
SSNs	87	80	20	40	40	50
Assault ships	65	50	50	50	50	82
SEALIFT						
Fast sealift ships	8	8	16	24	24	24
Afloat prepositioning ships	8	8	20	24	24	24
PERSONNEL (in thousands)						
Active	1,974	1,626	1,247	1,312	1,409	1,575
Reserve	1,176	920	666	691	904	933

Source: Congress, House, Committee on the Budget, *Funding and the Fiscal Year 1993 Budget* (Washington, DC: GPO, 1992), 45-46; *Department of Defense Annual Report to the President and the Congress* (Washington, DC: GPO, January 1991), 113.

TABLE 21. *Reductions from the fiscal year 1997 base force, alternative fiscal year 1997 force structures*

	Base Force Levels	Force A	Force B	Force C	Force D
ARMY					
Active divisions	12	-4	-4	-3	-2
Reserve division	6	-4	-4	0	0
Cadre divisions	2	-2	-2	-2	-2
MARINE CORPS					
Active divisions	2.33	-.33	-.33	-.33	.66
Reserve divisions	1	0	0	0	0
AIR FORCE					
Active wings	15	-9	-7	-5	-4
Reserve wings	11	-7	-5	-3	-2
NAVY					
Ships (total)	450	-230	-160	-110	-20
Carriers	13	-7	-5	-1	2
SSNs	80	-60	-40	-40	-30
Assault ships	50	0	0	0	+32
SEALIFT					
Fast sealift ships	8	+8	+16	+16	+16
Afloat prepositioning ships (beyond MPS)	8	+12	+16	+16	+16
PERSONNEL					
Active	1,626	-379	-314	-217	-51
Reserve	920	-254	-229	-16	+13

Source: Congress, House, Committee on the Budget, *National Defense Funding and the Fiscal Year 1993 Budget* (Washington, DC: GPO, 1992), 46.

TABLE 22. *Alternative defense plan budget authority reductions, fiscal years 1993-1997 (in billions of dollars)*

	FY 1997 Budget (Constant FY 1993 Dollars)	Cumulative FY 1993-97 Reductions
Force D	$255	-$15
FY 1993 (Bush program)	251	-43
Force C	234	-91
Force B	213	-164
Force A	200	-208

Source: Congress, House, Committee on the Budget, *National Defense Funding and the Fiscal Year 1993 Budget* (Washington, DC: GPO, 1992), 48.

Force C, however, promised stepped-up defense savings without explicitly surrendering military capabilities. Force C's projected five-year savings of approximately $90 billion below the FY 1992 baseline would allow Congress to preserve discretionary domestic spending, while providing sufficient forces for multiple contingencies and extended deployments. Furthermore, Force C active-duty personnel cuts, while approximately 15 percent greater than base force reductions, could be attained without significant numbers of involuntary separations, if implemented in equal stages over five years.[44] Active-duty levels much below Force C's would not only have required involuntary separations but would have necessitated implementing those separations fairly immediately.[45]

Nevertheless, proponents of the base force charged that the Force C option was deficient in terms of deterrence strategy and military capabilities. According to General Powell, "[The] Base Force . . . is better able [than Force C] to handle two major regional contingencies, is better able to handle a minor contingency should one occur, is better able to handle rotational ability."[46] Perhaps the clearest difference was that the base force provided a substantial forward presence to serve as the key to conventional deterrence.

The base force and Force C shared an emphasis on regional contingencies and threats and provided force structures to deal with concurrent contingencies and to sustain prolonged deployments. Both also claimed to provide effective strategic and conventional deterrence, but they differed in how best to deter potential enemies and, in the event deterrence failed, how best to respond. The base force depended heavily upon substantial forward deployments in major theaters around the world. As described by Secretary of Defense Cheney:

> The forward presence of U.S. forces will remain a key element of U.S. strategy, albeit at generally reduced levels, consistent with changing threats. Forces for forward presence are essential for strong security alliances. Forward-deployed forces play a critical role in deterring aggression, preserving regional stability, and protecting U.S. interests. They are visible evidence of U.S. commitment and provide our initial capability for crisis response and escalation control. This nation still very much depends on forward deployments in Asia, Europe, the Mediterranean, and the Atlantic, Pacific, and Indian Oceans. The United States must maintain forces sufficient to sustain those forward deployments and to reinforce them in the event of crisis.[47]

Base force advocates maintained that forward presence provided clear advantages if deterrence failed, facilitating crisis response and strengthening reinforcement and rotation capabilities. In addition, they claimed that the larger size and global deployment of the base force provided an enhanced capability to reconstitute forces in response to any major new threat. The base force's size and forward presence, noted General Powell, were in part a "hedge against the unknown."[48]

Still, Force C was neither presented nor perceived as a radical departure from the military spending and strategy assumptions of the base force program. Over 5 years, for example, Force C would cost less than the base force, but the projected differences were less than 5 percent. Under Force C and the base force, there would still be troops in Europe, although the size of the deployment under Force C would probably be half the projected 150,000 troop level under the base force. Under Force C and the base force, there would also be U.S. troops in Japan and South Korea, although here again the numbers deployed would be smaller.

These broad overlaps allowed Force C to serve as a politically safe alternative for Democrats who wanted to achieve greater defense savings than the Bush administration was proposing, and the fiscal approach of the Force C option was attractive to the Clinton campaign, which had from the beginning promised defense savings. In December 1991, Clinton had pledged unspecified, "cumulative savings" of $100 billion from the then-current Bush defense program. When Bush submitted his fiscal 1993 budget the following month, approximately $40 billion was cut from his previous defense program. The $60 billion gap that remained between the Bush and Clinton defense programs continued into and through the campaign but never emerged as a major campaign issue. Even if it had, Aspin's Force C plan was available to justify almost exactly the level of cuts Clinton had promised.

The Aspin plan was formulated well before Bill Clinton was finally nominated, but its approach was especially well suited to the "New Democrat" type of campaign Clinton waged. Indeed, during the campaign, Aspin twice met with Clinton to provide advice on defense issues, and, on September 21, Aspin gave a speech that discussed how Democrats should analyze the use of military force.[49] Three months later, Aspin was offered, and accepted, President-elect Clinton's invitation to be his nominee for Secretary of Defense.

The Clinton Defense Budgets

On February 17, 1993, the Clinton administration unveiled its economic recovery program and long-term budget plan. While detailed budget submissions for FY 1994 were delayed for several weeks, the initial budget blueprint made clear that defense reductions would be considerably higher than those proposed by Clinton during the campaign. For the fiscal year 1994-1998 period, the recommended defense cuts announced by Clinton were more than $125 billion below the Bush administration's budget submitted the previous year.[50] Indeed, the "official" cuts were understated by perhaps $30 billion, since they were measured against an adjusted defense spending baseline incorporating lower inflation and military personnel cost assumptions (table 23).

TABLE 23. *National defense functions budget authority projections, fiscal years 1993-1998 (in billions of dollars)*

	Fiscal Year					
	1993	1994	1995	1996	1997	1998
Original Bush budget (Jan 1992)	$280.9	$281.7	$284.4	$285.7	$290.6	NA
Adjusted Bush budget (Jan 1993)	274.3	275.5	278.0	278.3	284.6	293.4
Difference	-6.6	-6.2	-6.4	-7.4	-6.0	NA
Clinton budget (Feb 1993)	274.3	263.7	262.8	253.8	248.4	254.2
Clinton v. adjusted Bush	0.0	-11.8	-15.2	-24.5	-36.2	-39.2

Source: *National Journal* 25 (February 27, 1993): 517.

The defense budget reductions recommended by the administration were larger than expected, but their implications for defense policy or military strategy were not explored. Instead, the administration's defense spending program was discussed in the context of deficit reduction. The low priority assigned to substantive defense policy during the administration's first several months in office was underscored by the slow progress in filling civilian leadership positions in the Department of Defense.

By the end of March, only two of the 44 top political appointees in the Department were in place, and this leadership vacuum was accentuated by serious health problems affecting Defense Secretary Aspin.[51] Further muddying the defense debate was Clinton's decision, announced on January 25 to lift the ban on homosexuals in the military. The ensuing congressional uproar prompted Clinton to accept a 6-month delay in lifting the ban. Highly publicized committee hearings on the ban commenced in early April, at approximately the same time that congressional deliberations on the new defense spending program were beginning.[52] With all of these distractions, as well as the widespread preoccupation with deficit reduction, very little attention was paid to the unexpected size of the Clinton defense cuts.

Budgetary Constraints

On March 27, 1993, the Department of Defense finally unveiled its proposed FY 1994 budget. Described by Secretary Aspin as a "holding budget," the FY 1994 proposals incorporated neither the comprehensive bottom-up review nor the threat-based analysis that Aspin previously had deemed essential.[53] Instead, the FY 1994 defense plan followed the general outlines set forth by the previous administration, while cutting back force levels and weapons funding more rapidly.

The proposed spending levels in the FY 1994 budget, and the less detailed outyear projections, effectively canceled the base force defense program. What remained unclear were the force structure and military capabilities defining its replacement, but these considerations were of less immediate concern to the administration than were nondefense fiscal goals. In January 1993, the CBO had predicted, "Domestic discretionary spending is the category of spending that is most likely to benefit in the upcoming competition for funds within the 1994 and 1995 discretionary caps . . . as a result of President Clinton's stated interest in increasing government investments."[54]   It was therefore no surprise that the administration's proposed defense savings were sufficiently large to accommodate domestic spending increases within the discretionary caps.[55]

Defense savings were at the heart of the administration's deficit-reduction program.   The Clinton economic recovery program included more than $700 billion in deficit reduction for fiscal years 1994-1998, but proposed new spending for economic stimulus and investment programs lowered the net deficit reduction total to less than $500 billion.   Defense spending cuts and tax increases provided nearly three-fourths of the planned deficit reduction package (table 24).

Unlike defense, projected savings in nondefense spending usually stemmed from new or increased fees and taxes rather than actual spending cuts.   More than $20 billion in mandatory program reductions was accounted for by increasing the percentage of social security benefits subject to taxation, and nearly 10 percent of overall deficit reduction represented estimated interest savings resulting from lower deficits and improved debt management.   Program cuts, in sum, were restricted almost entirely to defense.

The differential treatment of defense and nondefense spending was underlined by the administration's decision to extend, rather than expand, budget process spending controls.[56] The administration recommended to Congress extending the Budget Enforcement Act's aggregate discretionary spending caps through FY 1998 and its pay-as-you-go controls on revenue policy and entitlements through FY 2003.[57] Maintaining aggregate discretionary caps would lock in deficit-reduction savings, while protecting the administration's domestic program initiatives. Extended pay-as-you-go controls similarly preserved deficit-reduction savings, but without necessitating rollbacks in major entitlements.   Under the Clinton administration's economic program and budget process prescriptions, defense was the only spending category in which sizable cuts were required.

TABLE 24. *Clinton administration initial deficit-reduction plan, fiscal years 1994-1998 (in billions of dollars)*

	Fiscal Year					
	1994	1995	1996	1997	1998	Total 1994-98
Baseline deficits	$301	$296	$297	$346	$390	$1,630
Defense discretion-ary	-7	-12	-20	-37	-36	-112
Nonde-fense (net)	+2	-6	-12	-22	-25	-64
Revenue increases (net)	-33	-34	-51	-68	-65	-251
Debt service interest	-0	-3	-7	-14	-22	-46
Net deficit reduction	-39	-54	-92	-140	-149	-473
Projected deficits	262	242	205	206	241	1,157

*Numbers may not add to totals because of rounding.
Source: Adapted from *Federal Budget Report* 12 (February 22, 1993): 4.

Congressional Action

In 1993, Congress moved through the initial stage of its budget process with unprecedented speed, adopting a concurrent budget resolution on April 1.[58] The congressional budget blueprint generally followed the administration's fiscal plan, but did include slightly higher deficit-reduction targets.[59] On defense, Clinton's 5-year spending recommendations were accepted with only minor changes (table 25).

The apparent consensus on spending obscured emerging policy disputes. Members of both the House and Senate Armed Services committees criticized the administration for

TABLE 25. *National defense spending levels, Clinton administration budget and congressional budget resolution, fiscal years 1994-1998 (in billions of dollars)*

Fiscal Year	Clinton Budget	Budget Resolution
1994		
Budget Authority	$263.4	$263.4
Outlays	276.9	277.0
1995		
Budget Authority	261.1	262.4
Outlays	270.8	272.1
1996		
Budget Authority	253.7	253.6
Outlays	264.7	264.7
1997		
Budget Authority	246.0	248.1
Outlays	246.8	248.9
1998		
Budget Authority	253.9	253.9
Outlays	252.5	252.4

Source: *Budget of the United States Government, Fiscal Year 1994* (Washington, DC: GPO), A-7, A-20; Congress, House, *Conference Report, Concurrent Resolution Setting Forth the Congressional Budget for the Fiscal Years 1994, 1995, 1996, 1997, and 1998* (Washington, DC: GPO, March 31, 1993), 5.

failing to identify which major weapons projects it wished to terminate in order to reduce FY 1994 weapons procurement funding by more than 15 percent below FY 1993 appropriations.[60] Aspin's successor as chairman of the House Armed

Services Committee, Ronald V. Dellums, complained that the failure to narrow procurement options reversed "hard-won understandings and policy positions reached by this committee and the Congress last year."[61] Dellums noted that "These [weapons] programs together are widely known to cost more than could have been afforded even within the Bush budget."[62]

There were also indications that the administration would face serious problems in preserving congressional support for its outyear defense spending requests. The House-passed budget resolution included higher multiyear defense cuts than did the Senate's, along with more than $25 billion in unspecified appropriations cuts that threatened to reduce defense even more. The Senate supported two defense-spending amendments to the budget resolution, both offered by Armed Services Committee chairman Sam Nunn, that sought to protect the defense budget against additional cuts. The first Nunn amendment provided for upward adjustments in outyear budgets if either inflation or federal pay growth proved higher than anticipated. The second provided that any future cuts below the Clinton administration's 5-year defense plan should go to deficit reduction rather than be transferred to domestic programs. These were non-binding amendments, in which the House did not concur. Nunn, who was one of only four Democrats to support an unsuccessful Republican initiative to reduce Clinton's recommended defense cuts by one-half, strongly criticized "those who seem to believe that the defense budget can bear all of the budget cuts."[63]

These skirmishes early in the year presaged intensifying conflicts over defense authorization and appropriations bills as defense reductions were implemented. When Aspin told the Senate Armed Services Committee that he would press for larger defense budgets if necessary, Nunn responded: "To cut defense, in this fiscal mood we're in now . . . is like falling off a log. To add back, short of some war-time scenario, is going to require extremely strong leadership."[64]

The Clinton Defense Program

The 5-year defense spending program introduced by President Clinton in 1993 marks an important downward shift in an already declining defense budget. Compared to the post-Cold War defense program of the Bush administration, the Clinton program is less costly, more than doubling the defense savings proposal by its predecessor. The Clinton spending plan also envisions a smaller active-duty force than the Bush base force, but the actual force levels and force structure that it can support remain uncertain.

Some of this uncertainty can be attributed to the priority assigned to deficit reduction at the beginning of Clinton's term. The administration and Congress negotiated an omnibus budget reconciliation package that achieved an estimated $500 billion in 5-year deficit savings, primarily through tax increases and discretionary spending limits. When Congress approved the reconciliation measure in August 1993, including the multiyear discretionary spending limits for defense and nondefense programs, it acted without having detailed proposals for future defense budgets. The Clinton administration had previously admitted that complete outyear requests would not be available until late 1993 or early 1994.[65] The spending limits for fiscal years 1994-1998 were thus adopted in a policy vacuum, making it difficult to assess what the Clinton administration and Congress had in mind for defense.

This uncertainty has been magnified by defense budget savings estimates that depend on optimistic, and questionable, assumptions about the economy and about congressional policy decisions. The Clinton administration ostensibly supports a 1.4 million active-duty force, but this force cannot possibly be funded at projected budget levels unless very large savings are realized from changes in military pay policies, proportional reductions in reserve forces, and other controversial policy initiatives.[66] Congress rejected a pay freeze in 1993, has opposed large reserve force reductions under Bush and Clinton, and could continue to block other policy-based savings that are necessary to avoid massive underfunding in the Clinton budgets.[67]

Just a few months after the FY 1994 budget was submitted to Congress, the Department of Defense disclosed that an additional $5.6 billion in outlays would have to be cut in order to offset what had proved to be inaccurate cost and policy assumptions.[68] In announcing these unforeseen cuts, Secretary of Defense Aspin declared, "I fully recognize the scope of the damage that reductions of this size could do to the capability and readiness of our forces. I will do everything in my power to keep this potential disaster from happening."[69] The danger of recurring underfunding crises, however, remains high given the admittedly precarious fit between the Clinton defense budgets and the 1.4 million active-duty force.

In an effort to resolve some of the more obvious tensions between its planned force levels and budgets, the Department of Defense has directed attention to its "bottom-up" review of defense programs. Early in this review process, which commenced during the spring of 1993, defense planners proposed a "win-hold-win" strategy that would permit the U.S. to avoid planning for two simultaneous regional wars and thereby to reduce costs. When this concept came under sharp attack, a "win-win" strategy was announced that restored the goal of fighting and winning two major regional wars at the same time. The fiscal impact of this upgraded strategic requirement was not explained, and the same issue was sidestepped when the Department of Defense decided to expand naval planning from a 10-carrier fleet to a 12-carrier fleet.[70] And while the 1993 defense planning review has identified a number of currently planned procurement programs for termination or large-scale rollbacks, planners have been instructed to ignore post-1999 modernization needs in order to keep within budget planning limits.[71]

There is widespread agreement that the force requirements of the Clinton administration defense program exceed its projected defense budgets, although there is substantial disagreement over the magnitude of the shortfall. When Secretary of Defense Aspin presented the initial Bottom-Up Review decisions in September 1993, he acknowledged a $13 billion multiyear shortfall.[72] Several months later, after Aspin's abrupt resignation and eventual replacement by William J. Perry, DOD officials had raised the estimated shortfall to $20 billion.[73] Congressional defense supporters have been considerably more pessimistic, citing underfunding estimates of as much as $50 billion over 5 years, and independent estimates have ranged as high as $20 billion annually by the end of the decade.[74] In any case, the administration's FY 1995 budget program does not address potential defense funding problems. The FY 1995 budget request for defense contains an adjustment to accommodate a congressionally mandated military pay raise, but the administration remains firmly committed to the multiyear defense spending program it proposed in 1993.

The Clinton administration is finding it difficult to fund the military capabilities it believes necessary within its own defense budget ceilings, and its quandary will deepen if Congress cuts these ceilings. There is some support among congressional Democrats to cut the defense budget faster and deeper than the Clinton administration has recommended, and this sentiment is likely to spread as the share of the budget to fund discretionary programs inexorably contracts. If Congress responds by taking an increasingly aggressive approach to the size and composition of the defense budget, funding shortages and policy oscillations will become even more severe than at present.

The Clinton administration, like the Bush administration, has adopted a budget policy strategy that jeopardizes defense needs. Spending controls to accomplish deficit reduction have been aimed at discretionary programs, while exempting the large entitlements. The discretionary spending ceilings under Bush and Clinton cannot accommodate domestic policy expansions without sizable defense cutbacks, which reinforces the congressional predisposition to transfer defense funds to domestic programs. Under the Bush administration, the base force was a legitimate and reasonably well-defined defense program that could be used to argue against proliferating defense transfers. The Clinton defense program is less well-defined, and defense budgets are accordingly much more open to transfer pressures. Whether the administration can establish a compelling case for its evolving defense program is far from being settled, but its task has been greatly complicated by the budget policy trends it has helped to solidify.

Notes

1. *Congressional Quarterly Weekly Report* 50 (October 17, 1992): 3254-55.

2. Ibid.

3. Ibid.

4. The 1972 presidential election featured especially sharp partisan divisions on defense spending, with Democratic nominee George S. McGovern's plan advocating a one-third cut in defense spending by fiscal 1975. From 1976-1988, the partisan differences were less stark, but in each instance Republican candidates advocated higher defense spending levels than their Democratic opponents were willing to support. The 1992 election was thus the first in several decades during which the candidates differed on the extent of defense cuts rather than defense growth.

5. *The Economic and Budget Outlook: An Update* (Washington, DC: Congressional Budget Office, 1992), 27.

6. Ibid., 28.

7. Ibid., 38.

8. Ibid., 42.

9. Congress, Senate, Committee on Armed Services, *Hearings, Threat Assessment, Military Strategy, and Defense Planning* (Washington, DC: GPO, 1992), 330-31.

10. Ibid., 526.

11. *Congressional Quarterly Weekly Report* 50 (August 22, 1992): 2569.

12. *Congressional Quarterly Weekly Report* 50 (July 18, 1992): 2108.

13. *Congressional Quarterly Weekly Report* 50 (October 17, 1992): 3254.

14. *Congressional Quarterly Weekly Report* 50 (June 27, 1992): 1901.

15. *Congressional Quarterly Weekly Report* 50 (October 17, 1992): 3253-54.

16. Congressional action on the trade agreement, which included reciprocal most-favored-nation status, was not completed until November 25, 1992.

17. *Congressional Quarterly Almanac, 1991* (Washington, DC: Congressional Quarterly Inc., 1992), 468.

18. Ibid.

19. Ibid.

20. Ibid.

21. Ibid., 470.

22. Ibid.

23. Ibid.

24. See Bob Woodward, "The Education of Les Aspin," *The Washington Post National Weekly Edition*, March 1-7, 1993, 8.

25. Congress, House, Committee on the Budget, *Hearing, National Defense Funding and the Fiscal Year 1993 Budget* (Washington, DC: GPO, 1992), 3.

26. Ibid., 3-4.

27. *Hearings, Threat Assessment*, 459-60.

28. Ibid., 460.

29. Woodward, 8.

30. *Hearing, National Defense Funding and the Fiscal Year 1993 Budget*, 12.

31. Ibid., 9-10.

32. Ibid., 3.

33. Ibid., 21.

34. Ibid., 22.

35. Ibid., 26-27.

36. Ibid., 25.

37. Ibid., 10-14.

38. Ibid., 14.

39. Ibid., 33.

40. Ibid., 34.

41. Ibid., 11.

42. Ibid.

43. Ibid., 39.

44. Ibid., 61.

45. Ibid., 61-62.

46. *Hearings, Threat Assessment*, 465.

47. *Report of the Secretary of Defense to the President and the Congress, January 1991* (Washington, DC: GPO, 1991), 4.

48. *Hearings, Threat Assessment*, 467.

49. Woodward, 8.

50. No detailed Bush administration budget was submitted for FY 1994. Instead, the administration issued a "perspective from which to evaluate choices and actions" in the form of a policy document titled *Budget Baselines, Historical Data, and Alternatives for the Future. Federal Budget Report* 12 (January 11, 1993): 1.

51. *Defense News,* March 22-28, 1993, 18.

52. The defense budget debate was further complicated by the base closure recommendations proposed by the Department of Defense on March 12. The proposals identified 31 major domestic bases for closure and 134 bases for cutbacks. *Congressional Quarterly Weekly Report* 51 (March 13, 1993): 616-18.

53. *The New York Times,* March 28, 1993, 14.

54. *The Economic and Budget Outlook: Fiscal Years 1994-1998* (Washington, DC: Congressional Budget Office, 1993), 45.

55. Ibid., 45-47.

56. The only significant exception was a request for "enhanced rescission authority" that was included in the administration's deficit-reduction package. This request, however, was a major retreat from the line-item veto authority Clinton had called for during the campaign.

57. *Federal Budget Report* 12 (February 22, 1993): 5. The final reconciliation measure extended the discretionary and pay-as-you-go controls through FY 1998.

58. Adoption of the FY 1994 congressional budget resolution was completed two weeks before the April 15 deadline. This adoption marked the first time in nearly two decades that Congress had complied with the statutory deadline.

59. The budget resolution changes from the original Clinton plan reflected political pressures for more spending cuts, particularly in light of Congressional Budget Office estimates that showed deficits under the Clinton program to be higher than the administration had initially forecast.

60. *Congressional Quarterly Weekly Report* 51 (April 3, 1993): 843-50.

61. Ibid., 843.

62. Ibid.

63. *National Journal* 25 (April 3, 1993): 823.

64. *Congressional Quarterly Weekly Report* 51 (April 3, 1993): 844.

65. *An Analysis of the President's February Budgetary Proposals* (Washington, DC: Congressional Budget Office, 1993), IV-1.

66. Ibid., IV-8.

67. Ibid. Of total projected defense savings, approximately 15 percent in budget authority reductions and 20 percent in outlay reductions were based upon pay freezes and other pay policy changes. In the 1993 budget reconciliation bill, Congress approved a military pay raise for fiscal 1994, rejecting the administration's proposed freeze on military and civilian pay for 1994.

68. *The New York Times,* June 10, 1993, A10.

69. Ibid.

70. *The New York Times*, August 11, 1993, 1, 9.

71. See *Defense News*, August 9-15, 1993, 1, 36.

72. *Defense News*, February 7-13, 1994, 44.

73. Ibid.

74. Ibid.

4. The Shrinking Discretionary Spending Margin

WHILE THE SHORT-TERM PROSPECTS for the defense budget are unfavorable under almost any scenario, the outlook for defense funding after the current round of post-Cold War reductions is ostensibly more optimistic. The fiscal 1994-1998 budget plans of the Clinton administration and Congress show 4 years of declining defense budget authority and outlay levels but then project modest increases in FY 1998. These budget programs, and Department of Defense planning, assume that funding and force levels can be stabilized once presently agreed upon defense savings are realized.

It is possible that the defense budget will be stabilized, particularly if a strategic consensus emerges. Widespread agreement between the executive branch and Congress on a national military strategy would certainly provide the defense budget with greater protection than it now enjoys against competing budgetary needs, but emerging budget policy trends will make it very difficult to arrest the decline in defense resources, even in a more supportive strategic environment. The most compelling of these interrelated trends are a spending policy dynamic and a structural deficit dynamic.

The share of the budget absorbed by automatic spending programs is large and certain to expand over the next decade. Because of this spending dynamic, the budgetary margin to support discretionary spending (defense and nondefense) will drop to uncommonly low levels. As spending policy has shifted toward nondiscretionary programs, structural deficits have mounted, and imposing deficits are likely to continue indefinitely. Even under highly optimistic economic and budget policy assumptions, projected structural deficits return to $200 billion levels by the end of the 1990s.[1]

These spending and deficit dynamics share a common cause—the enormous budgetary commitment necessary to support existing entitlements, particularly federal retirement and health programs. Retirement and healthcare entitlements have been largely immune from budget-cutting efforts, and their strong political support shows little sign of weakening. It seems inevitable that entitlement commitments must eventually be restricted in order to achieve sustainable fiscal policy, but until this occurs, discretionary programs, especially defense, will be forced to carry the entire burden of budgetary restraint.

Entitlements and the Spending Dynamic

The spending side of the federal budget is increasingly weighted toward nondiscretionary spending—entitlements and other forms of mandatory spending, along with interest payments on the federal debt. Just three decades ago, nondiscretionary spending accounted for approximately one-third of annual outlays, while discretionary programs accounted for roughly two-thirds (table 26). These budget shares have been reversed, and, by the late 1990s, nondiscretionary spending may account for as much as 70 percent of total federal outlays.

Much of the past growth in nondiscretionary spending has occurred in social welfare entitlements, such as social security, medicare, and medicaid. These programs are expected to maintain very high rates of growth in the future as demographic and economic factors raise the cost of retirement and healthcare benefits. Discretionary program growth has lagged well behind entitlement growth, and with tight discretionary spending limits in effect, the relative size of the discretionary budget will continue to decline. The spending constraints affecting defense, therefore, include the indirect effect of entitlement program growth, as well as the direct effect of competition with discretionary domestic needs. Indeed, the fate of the defense budget seems inextricably linked to the future course of entitlement policy.

Budget Process Controls

Entitlements provide payments or benefits to recipients whose eligibility is defined by law. The payment of benefits under an entitlement program is mandatory to those who qualify and

TABLE 26. *Discretionary and nondiscretionary budget shares, fiscal years 1962-1998*

Fiscal Year	Percentage of Total Outlays[*]	
	Nondiscretionary	Discretionary
1962	34%	66%
1965	35	65
1970	40	60
1975	54	46
1980	55	45
1985	58	42
1990	60	40
1995 (est.)	66	34
1998 (est.)	70	30

[*]Totals exclude offsetting receipts and deposit insurance outlays.

Source: *The Economic and Budget Outlook: Fiscal Years 1994-1998* (Washington, DC: Congressional Budget Office, 1993), 44, 128.

apply, and the legal rights of beneficiaries to payment have been repeatedly upheld by the courts. As a result, authorizations for entitlements are considered to be a "binding obligation . . . of the Federal Government."[2] Because appropriations to provide budget authority for entitlements are nondiscretionary, entitlements are usually funded through permanent appropriations. Although spending for entitlements cannot be directly controlled through the appropriations process, spending can be indirectly controlled through statutory changes in eligibility criteria and benefit formulas.

In circumventing direct appropriations control, entitlements pose more difficult spending-control problems than do discretionary programs. Once an entitlement is enacted, spending will continue automatically and indefinitely, and the only way to limit or to eliminate spending is for the president and majorities of the House and Senate to change the original authorizing legislation. Discretionary spending, by contrast, cannot take place unless the president and majorities of the House and Senate act affirmatively to appropriate the necessary budget authority for a given fiscal year.

In the absence of appropriations controls, special budgetary procedures have been established to deal with entitlements. Since the early 1980s, omnibus reconciliation legislation has been used on numerous occasions to achieve savings in various entitlement programs. Through special rules governing amendments, germaneness, and debate, the reconciliation process has allowed Congress to expedite action on comprehensive legislative measures that include entitlement program savings, as well as tax law changes, necessary to meet deficit-reduction targets.[3]

In addition, recent omnibus reconciliation legislation has imposed pay-as-you-go budget controls on entitlements. During a fiscal year, any new legislation affecting entitlement programs or tax policy must be, in the aggregate, deficit-neutral. An entitlement program increase or tax cut must be offset, either by a reduction in another entitlement or by an increase in another revenue source.[4] These pay-as-you-go controls are designed to make it more difficult to create new entitlements or to expand existing ones.

Even with these special procedures in place, policymakers have found it difficult to curb entitlement spending growth, particularly in programs that are sensitive to large-scale economic and demographic trends. Spending-control problems are further aggravated when entitlements are politically sacrosanct, serving large, well-organized beneficiary groups and resting upon strong ethical supports legitimizing government assistance.[5] As Wildavsky has noted, "Since the largest entitlements, especially the family of programs under social security, are the most sacrosanct, their growth overwhelms efforts to control their poorer cousins."[6]

The enormous budgetary impact associated with contemporary entitlement policy is largely attributable to several of these politically entrenched programs. Entitlement programs for the nonpoor have grown much more rapidly over the past two decades than have entitlement programs for the poor, with the social security and medicare programs accounting for much of this disparity. Among entitlements for the poor, medicaid is the only program with sustained long-term growth. With growth in federal spending largely reserved for social security, medicare, and medicaid, the resources available to support other programs appear destined to decline unless and until these entitlements are greatly curtailed.

Means-Tested Entitlements

Social welfare entitlements include means-tested and non-means-tested programs. The former consist of various public assistance programs to assist the poor, with benefits contingent upon need. The largest means-tested entitlements are medicaid, supplemental security income, food stamps, family support, and veterans' pensions.[7] In order to qualify for means-tested assistance, individuals must meet statutory limitations on income and other assets and must satisfy requirements related to age and family status. For non-means-tested programs, such as social security and medicare, there are no tests of financial need or financial assets, although other eligibility criteria must be met.

Both categories of federal social welfare programs were created by the Social Security Act of 1935. From the mid-1930s through the early 1960s, federal social welfare programs for the poor and nonpoor were gradually expanded. Eligibility and benefit levels were liberalized for public assistance programs, and the federal share of public assistance funding was periodically increased. Expansions in coverage and benefits were also enacted in the social security program.

By 1950, federal social welfare outlays had risen to approximately 5 percent of gross domestic product (GDP) and about one-third of total federal spending, although a large portion of this spending was devoted to education, medical care, and compensation benefits for veterans.[8] Outlays for public assistance programs totaled less than $1.5 billion in FY 1950, while social security and railroad retirement outlays were

115

just over $1 billion.[9] Over the next decade, the relative level of social welfare spending increased only slightly, although its composition began to shift toward social security and toward cash assistance for the poor. Since the early 1960s, the relative level of social welfare spending has more than doubled, but the growth in public assistance entitlements has been sporadic.

Public Assistance Expansion. Under Lyndon Johnson, the federal social welfare system was broadened to cover medical care for the poor (medicaid), permanent public assistance supplements for food, housing, and social services, and federal aid subsidies to education. Public assistance extensions were introduced to support federal antipoverty education, training, and employment programs. Federal matching funds for existing public assistance programs were increased, and the states were encouraged to liberalize their income-eligibility criteria.

The Johnson administration was unable, however, to establish a comprehensive, coordinated public assistance system. Instead, congressional opposition to "federalized welfare policy" forced the administration to follow a program-by-program approach. While a multitude of new and expanded programs emerged, congressionally authorized funding levels were usually well below those sought by the administration. As a result, the fiscal impact of the Great Society's public assistance initiatives did not fully emerge until after Johnson had left the presidency.

By 1970, spending for means-tested programs was 1 percent of GDP, only marginally higher than the pre-Great Society level (table 27). Social welfare outlays for the nonpoor were growing at a roughly similar rate. The increases in both categories of entitlements were primarily attributable to the new medicare and medicaid programs.

Even though this upward movement in social welfare spending was modest, it was decidedly unusual for a wartime budget. During World War II and Korea, the budget shares and GDP shares for social welfare outlays had declined sharply, as had real social welfare spending. The Vietnam War did not

TABLE 27. *Outlays for means-tested and non-means-tested entitlements, fiscal years 1962-1970 (as a percentage of GDP)*

	Percentage of GDP		
	Means-Tested	Non-Means-Tested	
Fiscal Year	Outlays	Outlays	Total
1962	0.8%	5.0%	5.8%
1963	0.8	4.9	5.7
1964	0.8	4.9	5.7
1965	0.8	4.6	5.4
1966	0.8	4.6	5.4
1967	0.8	5.2	6.0
1968	0.9	5.7	6.6
1969	0.9	5.7	6.6
1970	1.0	5.9	7.0

Source: *The Economic and Budget Outlook: Fiscal Years 1994-1998* (Washington, DC: Congressional Budget Office, 1993), 133.

have a similar restraining effect. Instead, social welfare entitlements continued to rise along with defense. Between fiscal years 1965 and 1970, entitlement outlays increased by $32 billion, while defense spending grew by $31 billion.[10]

This Vietnam spending anomaly did not receive much attention at the time, nor were its implications well understood. By the end of the Vietnam War, the defense budget as a percentage of GDP was at its lowest level since 1950. Although the GDP share for domestic spending, including entitlements and discretionary programs, was some 35 percent higher than pre-Vietnam levels, postwar domestic transfer pressures were so strong and antidefense sentiments so widespread that Congress imposed substantial real spending cuts on defense in order to expand domestic spending even further.

Growth and Retrenchment. The ensuing post-Vietnam surge in entitlement spending was pronounced. Over the FY 1970-1980 period, entitlement outlays quadrupled, rising from

7 percent of GDP to 11 percent. This overall growth, however, masked an emerging divergence between entitlements for the poor and the nonpoor.

During the early 1970s, virtually all public assistance entitlements were liberalized. Benefits and eligibility under the food stamp program were made more generous and then indexed in 1971.[11] Medicaid eligibility income limits were indexed 2 years later. A supplemental security income program (SSI) was initiated in 1973 to replace federal-state programs for the indigent aged, blind, and disabled, and its benefit levels were indexed the following year. These and other public assistance programs produced a rapid increase in spending, raising the GDP share of means-tested entitlements from 1.0 percent in FY 1970 to 1.7 percent 5 years later.

When the Carter administration took office, one of its highest priorities was social welfare reform. The 1976 Democratic platform had endorsed "comprehensive national health insurance with universal and mandatory coverage" and a guaranteed income scheme "both for the working poor and the poor not in the labor market."[12] Although the Carter administration enjoyed the ostensible support of large Democratic majorities in both houses of Congress, its efforts to enact these high-priority programs were repeatedly stymied by controversies over their potential costs and by the growing unpopularity of existing public assistance programs.

The social welfare policy debate of the late 1970s was eclipsed by cost issues, even though public assistance entitlements were a relatively minor contributor to the domestic spending buildup that was generating major budget-control problems. By focusing on public assistance costs, policymakers could avoid complicated and controversial programmatic issues such as welfare dependency, work incentives, family stability, and teenage pregnancy. Since their focus precluded a rigorous analysis of how to balance the social welfare needs of the poor and nonpoor, the comparative political weakness of programs serving the poor was reinforced.

The post-Vietnam surge in public assistance entitlements thus proved to be short-lived. By the end of the Carter presidency, public assistance outlays accounted for approximately the same percentage of GDP as they had at the tail end of the Ford presidency (table 28). In addition, cash assistance entitlements were declining relative to GDP, while non-cash, in-kind benefits for food, housing, and healthcare were increasing.[13] The ambitious plans of welfare reformers for a comprehensive public assistance system had been thwarted by fiscal and political obstacles that were to become even greater during the 1980s.

Ronald Reagan's social welfare agenda was, of course, very different from his predecessor's. The Reagan administration took office with a pledge to cut back federal domestic programs, particularly entitlements. Reagan's first set of budget proposals called for "preservation of the social safety net programs" constituting "an agreed-upon core of protection for the elderly, the unemployed, and the poor, and . . . the people who fought for the country in times of war."[14] Reagan's budget program went on to advocate revising "newer Federal entitlement programs," including "certain aspects of social safety net programs that have been added unnecessarily or have grown excessively."[15]

During Reagan's first year in office, public assistance eligibility restrictions and benefit reductions targeted coverage to those on the bottom of the income ladder. Benefits to the working poor were scaled back and, in some cases, eliminated under the revised AFDC and food stamp programs. Cutbacks were also instituted in housing, healthcare, and social services programs, as part of the Omnibus Budget Reconciliation Act of 1981.[16]

Reagan's proposals for additional public assistance cutbacks were repeatedly rebuffed by Congress, which later restored some of the program reductions enacted in 1981. Congress also rejected Reagan's 1982 "New Federalism" plan that would have turned the AFDC and food stamp programs entirely over to the states in exchange for full federal funding of medicaid. The administration and Congress did reach agreement on the Family Support Act of 1988, which signaled a shift in welfare policy from income assistance to preparation

TABLE 28. *Outlays for means-tested entitlements, fiscal years 1970-1980 (as a percentage of GDP)*

Fiscal Year	Medicaid	Percentage of GDP Other	Total
1970	0.3%	0.7%	1.0%
1971	0.3	1.0	1.3
1972	0.4	1.0	1.4
1973	0.4	0.9	1.3
1974	0.4	1.0	1.4
1975	0.5	1.2	1.7
1976	0.5	1.3	1.8
1977	0.5	1.2	1.7
1978	0.5	1.1	1.6
1979	0.5	1.1	1.6
1980	0.5	1.2	1.7

Source: *The Economic and Budget Outlook: Fiscal Years 1994-1998* (Washington, DC: Congressional Budget Office, 1993), 133.

and training for work. Mandatory training and work requirements were imposed as a condition for AFDC benefits, child support enforcement was strengthened, and states were allowed to require that minor parents receiving AFDC benefits live with their parents or other adult relatives.

Under the Reagan administration, medicaid was the only major component of public assistance spending to show a relative increase (table 29). By the end of Reagan's tenure, cash assistance and other non-healthcare outlays were approximately 1 percent of GDP, which was about the same level as during the early 1970s. Moreover, cash assistance outlays were, in relative terms, close to pre-Great Society levels despite the considerably larger number of beneficiaries.

Neither the Bush administration nor the Clinton administration has renewed Reagan's attack on public assistance spending, although each has advocated "welfare reform." The escalating growth of medicaid, however, has frustrated efforts to revise public assistance policy. The Clinton

TABLE 29. *Outlays for means-tested entitlements, fiscal years 1980-1990 (as a percentage of GDP)*

| | | Percentage of GDP | |
Fiscal Year	Medicaid	Other	Total
1980	0.5%	1.2%	1.7%
1981	0.6	1.3	1.8
1982	0.6	1.2	1.8
1983	0.6	1.2	1.8
1984	0.5	1.1	1.7
1985	0.6	1.1	1.7
1986	0.6	1.1	1.7
1987	0.6	1.0	1.6
1988	0.6	1.0	1.7
1989	0.7	1.0	1.7
1990	0.8	1.1	1.8

Source: *The Economic and Budget Outlook: Fiscal Years 1994-1998* (Washington, DC: Congressional Budget Office, 1993), 133.

administration's proposed 2-year limit on public assistance benefits, for example, is linked to an expansion of job training and services that would entail additional short-term costs, but projected medicaid spending increases will make it extremely difficult to finance these additional costs or to expand other non-healthcare benefit programs.

Over the past three decades, medicaid has emerged as the costliest form of public assistance. Over the next decade, under current policy, the imbalance between medicaid and other public assistance programs will become even more pronounced (table 30). In addition, projected medicaid growth is likely to boost total public assistance spending to over 3 percent of GDP, which would be the highest level in the history of public assistance entitlements.

The looming fiscal impact of public assistance entitlements is not a consequence of wholesale legislative expansions but

TABLE 30. *Baseline outlay projections for means-tested entitlements, fiscal years 1992-1998**

| | Fiscal Year | | | | | | | |
	1992	1993	1994	1995	1996	1997	1998	Increase
Medicaid	$68	$76	$88	$100	$112	$125	$139	$71
Food stamps	23	25	25	25	26	27	28	5
Supplemental security income	18	21	25	24	24	29	31	13
Family support	16	17	17	18	18	19	20	4
Veterans' pensions	4	3	3	3	3	3	3	-1
Child nutrition	6	6	7	7	8	8	9	3
Earned income tax credit	8	10	11	16	19	22	22	14
Stafford loans	2	2	2	2	2	2	2	0
Other	3	3	3	3	4	4	4	1
Total	148	163	182	200	216	238	258	+110

*Fiscal year 1992 is actual outlays. Fiscal years 1993-1998 are estimates.
Source: *The Economic and Budget Outlook: An Update* (Washington, DC: Congressional Budget Office, 1993), 41.

122

rather of increased spending for medicaid. Federal medicaid costs have continued to climb despite recurrent legislative attempts to control federal healthcare expenditures and to shift a greater portion of medicaid financing to the states. These efforts have been frustrated by the growing number of medicaid beneficiaries and by the seemingly inexorable climb of healthcare costs. While public assistance entitlements have had a limited effect on discretionary spending in the past, medicaid is likely to inflate this effect in the future. The medicaid program is so large and growing so fast that its growth will likely necessitate spending cutbacks elsewhere in the budget.

Non-Means-Tested Entitlements

Three decades ago, outlays for all non-means-tested entitlements accounted for about 3 percent of GDP. Current outlays for non-means-tested entitlements are climbing toward 10 percent of GDP, and projected outlays will exceed that level by the end of the decade. Among nonpoor entitlements, spending for three types of programs—social security, medicare, and other federal retirement and disability programs—has produced much of the past growth and, under existing policy, will generate virtually all of the future growth. By the late 1990s, federal retirement and associated healthcare outlays could account for as much as 40 percent of the federal spending budget.[17]

Social security ranks as the largest federal spending program, having surpassed defense during FY 1993. The medicare program is less than one-half the size of social security, but the disparity between the two is shrinking because of medicare's higher growth rate. Medicare spending growth averaged 10 percent annually over the past decade and is expected to increase to nearly 15 percent annually over the fiscal 1993-1998 period.[18] The federal government's other retirement and disability programs are much smaller than social security or medicare, and their projected growth is considerably less. Several non-means-tested entitlements, including unemployment compensation, veterans' benefits, and farm price

123

supports, are expected to have no growth or even to decline slightly over the near term.[19] In terms of budgetary impact, then, the family of programs under the social security system is by far the most important.

Program Extensions. From 1935 to 1965, numerous amendments were added to the Social Security Act.[20] Coverage was broadened to include dependents and survivors of covered workers and to encompass approximately 90 percent of the workforce. Disability benefits were established for workers below retirement age and financed through a separate trust fund. Early retirement benefits, at age 62, were made available to women in 1956 and to men in 1961. Benefit levels were also periodically raised, with average monthly benefits per worker more than tripling between 1939 and 1964.

In order to finance higher benefits and broadened eligibility, social security taxable earnings limits and tax rates had to be raised frequently (table 31). By the mid-1960s, annual social security tax revenues were running at approximately $17 billion, although the maximum tax on employees was still under $200 per year. Social security trust fund surpluses were sufficient to cover more than 15 months of benefit payments.[21]

Perhaps the most important policy conflict during the social security system's first three decades of operation was over healthcare benefits. When the Roosevelt administration proposed the social security system, it endorsed the eventual inclusion of national health insurance for the elderly. The administration never submitted national health legislation to Congress, however, nor did it actively support national health initiatives introduced by congressional Democrats.[22] The Truman administration was more resolute in its advocacy of a comprehensive health insurance program financed through social security taxes, but its proposals were rejected by Congress. In 1950, Congress enacted a limited program of federal reimbursements to the states to finance health vendor payments for persons on public assistance and, 10 years later, a similar plan was approved for the medically needy aged. While federal reimbursement formulas were subsequently raised for both programs, a comprehensive medical insurance program for the aged was not enacted until 1965.

The 89th Congress' huge Democratic majorities quickly approved a medical care program for the aged that was even broader than the initial program sponsored by the Johnson administration. The medicare program, as contained in the 1965 omnibus social security bill, provided for social security tax financing of basic healthcare benefits for the aged (hospital care, nursing home care, certain outpatient diagnostic services, and home healthcare services) and for a supplemental insurance plan (financed by participants' premiums and taxpayers' funds) to cover physicians' fees and other healthcare services.

TABLE 31. *Social Security taxable earnings base and tax rate, 1937 to 1963 (employee and employer respectively)*

Year	Taxable Earnings Base	Tax Rate	Maximum Tax
1937	$3,000	1.0 %	$30.00
1950	3,000	1.5	45.00
1951	3,600	1.5	54.00
1954	3,600	2.0	72.00
1955	4,200	2.0	84.00
1957	4,200	2.25	94.50
1959	4,800	2.5	120.00
1960	4,800	3.0	144.00
1962	4,800	3.125	150.00
1963	4,800	3.625	174.00

Source: Compiled by author.

Funding Growth. Between 1965 and 1975, social security and medicare spending rose sharply, climbing above 5 percent of GDP in 1975. This growth was spurred by larger than anticipated costs for the newly enacted medicare program and by a series of social security benefit increases enacted by Congress. After a 7 percent social security benefit increase in 1965, additional increases were passed in 1967 (13 percent), 1969 (15 percent), 1971 (10 percent), and 1972 (20 percent). In 1972, social security benefits were indexed to the consumer price index (CPI), effective in 1975. An additional benefit increase of 11 percent was passed in 1973, and the timetable was advanced for scheduled cost-of-living adjustments (COLAs).

There were other sources of social security spending growth during this period, including an expansion in the beneficiary population from 20.9 million in 1965 to 31.9 million in 1975.[23] The escalation in social security program costs, however, was unusually high when compared to the number of beneficiaries, to inflation, or to economic growth.[24] Social security outlays were also outpacing revenues, despite rapidly increasing social security tax liabilities for employees and employers. The social security trust funds began to run deficits in FY 1976, and the Social Security Board of Trustees' annual report for 1977 forecast continuing depletion of reserves, with the disability insurance trust fund being exhausted in 1979 and the old age and survivors trust fund running out 4 years later.[25]

In 1977, the Carter administration and Congress attempted to replenish the trust funds through a massive social security tax increase, totaling $227 billion over 10 years. Under the wage base and tax rate increases scheduled for 1977-1987, maximum social security taxes for employees and for employers would climb from less than $1,000 to more than $3,000.[26] The social security amendments of 1977 contained a technical adjustment in the existing benefit formula, but no major benefit reductions were adopted for either current or future retirees.[27] Instead, social security's funding problems were attacked exclusively on the revenue side.

During this period, medicare outlays were rising, although less impressively than social security's. Between fiscal years 1965 and 1980, medicare grew by less than $35 billion, while social security spending increased by $100 billion. Given the overwhelming opposition in Congress to cutbacks in social security benefits, the prospects for retrenchment in the less costly medicare benefits were nonexistent.

By 1980, non-means-tested entitlement outlays had climbed to well over 9 percent of GNP, with social security and medicare accounting for more than 60 percent of this total (table 32). During the 1970s, largely as a result of social security benefit increases, real income for the elderly had grown by 23 percent, while there had been no real income growth for the general population.[28] Social security benefit increases had helped to reduce the poverty rate among the elderly by nearly 40 percent, with an even steeper decline in the poverty rate when noncash benefits, particularly medicare, were taken

TABLE 32. Outlays for non-means-tested entitlements, fiscal years 1965-1980 (as a percentage of GDP)

Fiscal Year	Social Security	Medicare	Other Retirement/ Disability	Unemployment Compensation	Farm Price Supports	Other	Total
1965	2.5%	.0%	0.5%	0.4%	0.4%	0.7%	4.6%
1966	2.7	*	0.6	0.3	0.2	0.8	4.6
1967	2.7	0.4	0.6	0.3	0.2	0.9	5.2
1968	2.7	0.6	0.7	0.3	0.4	1.1	5.7
1969	2.9	0.7	0.6	0.2	0.5	0.8	5.7
1970	3.0	0.7	0.7	0.3	0.4	0.9	5.9
1971	3.3	0.7	0.8	0.5	0.3	0.9	6.6
1972	3.4	0.7	0.8	0.6	0.4	1.1	7.0
1973	3.8	0.7	0.9	0.4	0.3	1.5	7.5
1974	3.9	0.8	1.0	0.4	0.1	1.5	7.7
1975	4.2	0.9	1.2	0.8	*	2.0	9.2
1976	4.3	1.0	1.1	1.1	0.1	1.9	9.5
1977	4.4	1.1	1.1	0.7	0.2	1.5	9.0
1978	4.3	1.1	1.1	0.5	0.3	1.7	8.9
1979	4.2	1.2	1.1	0.4	0.1	1.5	8.6
1980	4.4	1.3	1.2	0.6	0.1	1.6	9.3

* Less than 0.05 percent.

Source: The Economic and Budget Outlook: Fiscal Years 1994-1998 (Washington, DC: Congressional Budget Office, 1993), 133.

127

into account.[29]

The maturation of the social security system during the 1960s and 1970s had a very positive impact on the economic well-being of the elderly, but since no efforts were made to target benefits, the fiscal repercussions were enormous. Received benefits greatly outpaced contributions (plus interest) for all income classes among retirees, with the transferstaxpayers to beneficiaries accounting for more than three-fourths of total benefit payments.[30] Replacement rates and benefit formulas for low-income retirees were more generous than for high-income retirees, but actual dollar transfers to the latter group were larger.[31] Finally, the improvement in life expectancy by the end of the 1970s meant that workers could expect to recover all of their social security "investment" in approximately 5 years and to receive an additional 12 years of "unearned" benefits.[32]

Retrenchment Efforts. The Carter administration made no effort to redirect or target nonpoor entitlements. The social welfare agenda of the Reagan administration, by contrast, included a direct attack on "benefits for people with middle to upper incomes."[33] Reagan's initial budget program, submitted to Congress less than 2 months after he took office, set out "clear, consistent, and economically sound criteria . . . for evaluating claims for Federal support."[34] These criteria included the "revision of entitlements to eliminate unintended benefits" and the "reduction of benefits for people with middle to upper incomes."[35] The Reagan budget emphasized that this latter criterion "directly challenges the drift toward the universalization of social benefit programs."[36]

During the spring of 1981, with the Social Security trust funds facing another financial crisis, the Reagan administration proposed significant cutbacks in benefits. Its most controversial proposals included: (1) a reduction in benefits for early retirees (age 62); (2) a less generous benefit formula for future retirees; (3) more stringent eligibility requirements for disability benefits; and (4) a 3-month delay in the annual COLA benefit increase.[37] Additional savings were to be achieved by eliminating the minimum social security benefit floor and by basing benefits solely on prior earnings.

The political response to the Reagan initiatives was heated and swift. The Republican-controlled Senate narrowly defeated, by a vote of 49-48, an amendment to a supplemental appropriations bill that denounced the Reagan proposals as "a breach of faith with those aging Americans who have contributed to the Social Security system" and vowed opposition to "precipitously and unfairly" reducing early retirement benefits.[38] The Senate did adopt, by a unanimous vote, an amendment that promised to protect early retirement benefits and to reject any wholesale social security program changes.

Less than 2 weeks later, the administration backed down, announcing that the President was "not wedded to any single solution."[39] While Congress agreed to repeal the minimum social security benefit as part of the 1981 omnibus budget reconciliation bill, it rejected outright less generous social security benefit formulas or reduced early retirement benefit levels. Later in the year, the minimum benefit was restored for current retirees, and borrowing was authorized among the social security trust funds in order to buttress the depleted old-age and survivors (OASI) trust fund.

In 1983, Congress and the administration agreed to a comprehensive social security rescue plan designed to solve the immediate and the long-term solvency problems facing the trust funds. The plan was based on recommendations issued by a bipartisan National Commission on Social Security Reform that had been appointed in late 1981 by President Reagan and congressional leaders. The basic issue facing the Commission, and Congress, was whether tax hikes or benefit cuts should bear the greater burden in restoring the social security system's solvency. The perception that benefit cuts were politically riskier finally prevailed, and Congress approved a plan that immediately generated additional revenues by raising payroll taxes for both employers and employees and by mandating social security coverage for all federal employees. No direct benefit cuts were enacted, although a COLA delay of 6 months was adopted, and social security benefits of high-income recipients were made subject to partial taxation. In addition, the retirement age for full benefits was raised to 66 in 2007 and to 67 in 2027, with early retirement benefits scaled back at these times as well.[40]

The Social Security Amendments of 1983 instituted a partial advanced funding system intended to build sufficient trust fund reserves to finance benefits for current workers retiring in the next century. Social security taxes, therefore, were set well above levels needed to fund benefits for current retirees. The social security tax rate for employees and employers was raised from 6.7 percent in 1983 to 7.65 percent in 1990 and maximum taxable earnings were indexed based on a 1983 level of $37,800.[41] From 1980 to 1990, the maximum social security tax for employees and employers would increase by an estimated 250 percent, to just under $4,000, to fund current and future benefits.

The social security rescue plan eliminated the social security benefit issue from the deficit-control agenda, an exclusion that was formalized when the 1985 and 1987 Gramm-Rudman-Hollings balanced-budget bills removed the main social security trust funds from the unified budget and exempted them from any automatic spending cuts and from the reconciliation process.[42] While social security COLA delays were occasionally debated during the mid-1980s, neither the Reagan administration nor Congress was willing to reconsider benefit cuts. As a result, social security outlays more than doubled during the 1980s, and social security taxes rose even faster. The Reagan administration obviously had failed to achieve its original goal of curbing social security spending and, more important, had agreed to a financing plan that would preserve high, universal benefits into the next century.

Medicare policy during the 1980s attracted sustained attention from the administration and Congress, although, in the end, the basic structure of the medicare program remained intact. The medicare trust funds, like those for social security retirement benefits, encountered serious financial difficulties during the early 1980s, as rapidly rising healthcare costs pushed up medicare spending. For years, healthcare cost increases had outpaced what were unusually high overall inflation rates, and the disparity in 1981 (12.5 percent for medical care inflation versus 8.9 percent for overall inflation) spurred legislative efforts to impose cost controls on healthcare providers.[43]

The 1981 omnibus budget reconciliation bill included limits on medicare reimbursements for hospital services and home health services. In 1983, a new "prospective-payment system" was established for hospitals as part of the medicare section of the social security bill. In 1984, limits and restrictions on physicians' fees were enacted. Reconciliation legislation during Reagan's second term followed this same approach of cutting payments to hospitals and physicians in order to restrain medicare spending increases.

Medicare benefits and coverage, however, were largely immune from cost-cutting efforts. Early in Reagan's first term, deductibles for medicare benefits were raised slightly, as were premiums for medicare Part B insurance (supplementary insurance available to medicare beneficiaries to cover physicians' services). The latter change was designed to reduce the growing shortfall between premium revenues and Part B costs. Premiums were increased in order to cover 25 percent of Part B spending, with the remainder financed by general revenues. Legislation has since provided for additional premium increases to maintain the 25-75 percent ratio, but the medicare Part B subsidy remains quite high for all beneficiaries, regardless of income.[44]

The extreme reluctance among members of Congress to consider reductions in medicare benefits was underscored by their response to media reports in 1982 that the Reagan administration was considering proposals for means-testing medicare eligibility and benefits. No formal proposal was ever submitted, but Congress adopted an amendment to an FY 1983 appropriations bill declaring its opposition to "any proposal to impose a 'means test' on eligibility for the Medicare program or benefits provided by the Medicare program."[45] Congress later rejected proposals to base Part B premiums on beneficiaries' incomes and to increase and to index Part B deductibles.[46]

With medicare benefits protected and heavily subsidized

and medicare spending continuing to rise sharply, the solvency of the medicare trust fund has become a serious concern. In the 1990 budget reconciliation bill, Congress raised the ceiling on earnings subject to the medicare portion of the social security tax (1.45 percent) from $51,300 to $125,000 in 1991 and provided for annual adjustments equal to the social security wage base increase. Projected revenues from lifting the medicare wage cap were $27 billion for fiscal years 1991-1995, the largest single revenue increase contained in the reconciliation bill.[47] In the 1993 budget reconciliation bill, the medicare payroll tax wage cap was lifted entirely, adding $30 billion in estimated revenue gains for fiscal years 1994-1998. These revenue increases have boosted trust fund reserve projections, but medicare benefit levels still pose a continuing financing challenge.[48]

Since 1980, notwithstanding numerous efforts to control healthcare costs, the average annual rate of real growth in medicare outlays has been the highest among major categories of federal spending.[49] Disproportionately high growth is expected to persist, with the projected rate of real growth per medicare enrollee averaging 5.7 percent annually for the Part A (hospital insurance) program during fiscal years 1993-1998 and 9.7 percent for the Part B (supplementary medical insurance) over the same period.[50]As noted by the CBO, "Clearly, controlling total spending for health and reducing the federal budget deficit will be difficult if current trends in national health expenditures continue."[51]

Spending Projections

The federal budget will become even more heavily weighted toward social security, medicare, and medicaid over the next decade, unless there are immediate and far-reaching policy cutbacks. Total spending for entitlements and other mandatory programs (excluding deposit insurance) is projected at $1.035 trillion in FY 1998, a net increase of $323 billion over actual spending in FY 1992 (table 33). Nearly all of this increase will occur in social security (+$106 billion), medicare (+$110 billion), and medicaid (+$71 billion). Discretionary spending, by comparison, will be flat over this period.

The remaining nondiscretionary spending category, net interest outlays, is expanding as well, with an estimated increase of more than $50 billion over the fiscal 1992-1998 period. By fiscal year 1998, net interest and the three largest entitlement programs could account for nearly 60 percent of total federal spending, compared to less than 50 percent in FY 1992. Between fiscal years 1992 and 1998, net interest and the three largest entitlements will have absorbed 95 percent of the net spending growth in the federal budget.

The constricting effect of nondiscretionary spending growth on the discretionary portion of the budget shows no sign of abating. According to the GAO, combined current policy outlays for social security, medicare, and medicaid could increase by as much as 5 percentage points of GNP by 2020, with medicare and medicaid growing especially rapidly.[52] While current policy will presumably be changed to avoid this outcome, even less imposing growth would inevitably tighten discretionary spending margins.

Policymakers may eventually find themselves with no choice but to limit retirement and healthcare benefits in order to control entitlement spending, but these decisions cannot be implemented easily or quickly. The spending dynamic that is rooted in entitlement policy cannot be reversed over the next several years or perhaps even the next decade. As a consequence, entitlement spending will continue to generate large structural deficits.

The Deficit Dynamic

The budget deficit, which is the difference between the federal government's revenues and spending during a fiscal year, can be measured in several different ways. The unified budget deficit comprises all federal revenues and spending, including the social security trust funds. On-budget deficits, which were used prior to 1967 and have been reinstituted recently, exclude the social security trust funds (and the Postal Service).[53] Because the federal budget's spending and revenues are so

TABLE 33. *Baseline entitlement and discretionary program outlays, fiscal years 1992-1998 (in billions of dollars)*

	Fiscal Year*				
Programs	1992	1994	1996	1998	Increase
Means-Tested Programs					
Medicaid	$68	$88	$112	$139	+$71
All other	80	94	104	119	+39
Total	148	182	216	258	+110
Non-Means-Tested Programs					
Social Security	285	319	354	391	+106
Medicare	129	160	196	239	+110
Subtotal	414	479	550	630	+216
All other	151	147	135	148	-3
Total	565	626	685	778	+213
Total Mandatory Spending					
	712	808	901	1,035	+323
Total Discretionary Spending					
	536	542	548	547	+11

*Fiscal year 1992 is actual outlays. Fiscal years 1994-1998 are estimates based on baseline policy projections. Spending includes benefits only, not administrative costs.

Source: *The Economic and Budget Outlook: An Update* (Washington, DC: Congressional Budget Office, 1993), 38, 41.

sensitive to the state of the economy, the structural or standardized employment deficit measure removes the effects of economic cycles on the government's finances.[54] The structural deficit represents the imbalance between spending policy and revenue policy when the economy is operating at full potential growth.

Since recent deficit levels are impressive regardless of the specific measure used, it may not seem to make a great deal of difference which is employed (table 34). Although there are policy biases associated with each, the on-budget deficit measure is especially problematical. The on-budget deficit distinguishes between the social security trust funds and the remainder of the budget in order to shield the social security program from changes that would diminish planned surpluses and curtail the reserves needed to help finance benefits for the post-2010 retirement generation. Removing social security from the unified budget also imposes a disproportionate burden on other programs, particularly defense and nondefense discretionary spending, to balance artificially large on-budget deficits.

As the CBO has emphasized, treating social security or any of the more than 150 federal trust funds as self-supporting and therefore separable from the rest of the budget is inaccurate and misleading:

> First, no large federal program is truly self-supporting, whether it is labeled a trust fund program or whether (like defense or Medicaid) it lacks this label. Trust fund receipts come from taxing one group, such as current workers, to confer benefits on others, such as retirees; in other words, the programs are redistributive. And much of their income, in fact, simply comes from transfers within the budget. Such transfers shift money from the general fund (boosting the federal funds deficit) to trust funds (swelling the trust fund surplus). . . . Without such transfers, the trust funds would exhibit deficits, not surpluses.
>
> The second reason is more compelling, setting trust funds aside . . . can distort budget decisionmaking. The same economic pie, namely GDP, supports trust fund programs and other programs alike. Putting trust fund programs on a favored footing shifts the onus of deficit reduction to other programs that lack this protective label. Sound decisionmaking, by contrast, demands that spending and revenue proposals be evaluated on their merits and not their labels.[55]

The unified deficit is a more accurate representation of budget policy and of the budget's impact on credit markets and the economy, while the structural deficit indicates the dimensions

135

TABLE 34. *Federal budget deficit under alternative measures, fiscal years 1977-1992 (in billions of dollars)*

Fiscal Year	Unified Deficit	On-Budget Deficit	Standardized Employment Deficit
1977	$53.7	$49.8	$38.4
1978	59.2	54.9	55.3
1979	40.2	38.2	42.7
1980	73.8	72.7	47.7
1981	79.0	74.0	37.4
1982	128.0	120.1	46.7
1983	207.8	208.0	105.2
1984	185.4	185.7	133.1
1985	212.3	221.7	177.4
1986	221.2	238.0	184.7
1987	149.8	169.3	118.9
1988	155.2	194.0	151.2
1989	212.3	205.2	145.7[*]
1990	221.4	278.0	161.0[*]
1991	269.5	321.7	179.8[*]
1992	290.2	340.3	201.5[*]
Annual Average	$156.2	$173.2	$114.2

[*]Excludes deposit insurance.

Source: *Reducing the Deficit: Spending and Revenue Options* (Washington, DC: Congressional Budget Office, 1993), 4.

of budget policy changes (revenue increases and spending cuts) needed to reduce or eliminate deficits and neutralize their economic effects. Concern with deficits, and with their political and economic effects, is not a uniquely modern preoccupation. According to a leading study, "From the earliest days of the republic the idea of balancing the federal government's budgets has played a central role in American political life."[56] Still, the dimensions of contemporary deficit problems dwarf those of earlier periods.

The Deficit Buildup

The New Deal marked a turning point in the history of deficit control. From 1789-1930, the federal budget was usually balanced, although wars and economic crises resulted in occasional large deficits. During the 1920s, for example, federal spending declined by 50 percent, the budget was balanced each year, and accumulated surpluses reduced the $23 billion World War I debt by more than one-third. Prior to the New Deal, the operative rule of federal budget policy was that budgets should be balanced, except under truly unusual circumstances, and that any debts that were incurred should be retired as quickly as possible.

The New Deal inaugurated an era during which fiscal stimulus policies have made deficits acceptable and spending commitments have made them commonplace. Since the early 1930s, the budget has been in deficit for all but 9 years, and the current series of uninterrupted deficits goes all the way back to FY 1969 (table 35). Deficits have been growing quite rapidly, in current dollars and in constant dollars, during peacetime and wartime, during recessions and recoveries, and during Democratic and Republican administrations.

The recent deficit buildup has also outpaced economic growth. During the 1950s and 1960s, deficits averaged less than 1 percent of GDP. After the Vietnam War, this average moved upward, climbing above 4 percent during the 1980s and reaching even higher levels during the early 1990s. This escalation in peacetime deficits has caused a parallel surge in the accumulated federal debt. The publicly-held debt now

137

TABLE 35. *Federal budget deficits, fiscal years 1930-1994 (in billions of dollars)*

Fiscal Years	Number of Deficits	Current Dollars		Constant Dollars (FY 1987)
		Net Deficits*	Annual Average	Annual Average
1930-39	9	$20.9	$2.1	NA
1940-49	7	177.6	17.8	154.5
1950-59	7	17.4	1.7	7.9
1960-69	8	56.5	5.6	21.0
1970-79	10	365.0	36.5	70.5
1980-89	10	1,566.0	156.6	159.1
1990-94 (est.)	5	1,298.0	260.0	NA

*Total deficits minus total surpluses; administrative budget basis for fiscal years 1930-34; unified budget basis for fiscal years 1935-1994.

Source: *Supplement, Budget of the United States Government, Fiscal Year 1993, Part Five* (Washington, DC: GPO, 1992), 17-18; *The Economic and Budget Outlook: An Update* (Washington, DC: Congressional Budget Office, 1993), 38.

stands at more than $3 trillion, compared to less than $300 billion in FY 1970 (figure 3). Further, the post-World War II decline in publicly-held debt as a percentage of GDP ended during the 1970s, and the level has since climbed to over 50 percent. While the U.S. economy supported even higher relative debt levels after World War II, those levels began to drop as postwar spending declined. The recent upsurge promises to continue for quite some time, because burgeoning nondiscretionary spending commitments are causing added deficits and debt.

The economic impact of this deficit and debt record may be

hotly disputed, but the budgetary effects are unmistakably clear.[57] With both interest rates and debt levels having moved upward over the past two decades, the costs of financing the debt have soared. Since 1970, annual net interest outlays have

FIGURE 3. *Federal debt held by the public, fiscal years 1940-1992 (in billions of dollars and as a percentage of GDP)*

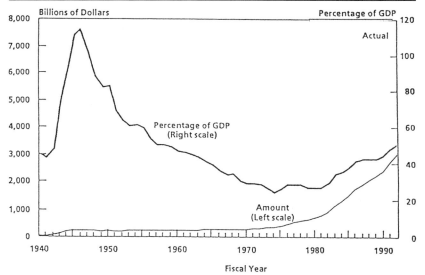

Source: *Federal Debt and Interest Costs* (Washington, DC: Congressional Budget Office, 1993), 2.

increased from less than $15 billion to over $200 billion (figure 4). With projected net interest outlays remaining above 3 percent of GDP, this drain on the federal budget will persist indefinitely.

Projected Deficits

While projections of future deficit and debt levels are unsure, there is little reason to expect any substantial near-term improvement. The 1990 budget agreement, which contained nearly $500 billion in deficit-reduction savings, projected that the

139

deficit would drop from $250 billion in FY 1991 to $29 billion in FY 1995. Instead, the FY 1995 deficit is currently estimated at nearly $200 billion, and the FY 1992-1994 deficits are also proving to be much larger than anticipated. The Clinton administration's 1993 deficit-reduction package includes another $500 billion in estimated savings, but assumes that deficits will remain quite high (about $200 billion in FY 1998) even if the revenue increases and spending reductions in the package are fully realized.

The deficit-reduction problem is accordingly enormous and chronic. As table 36 shows, baseline deficits are projected at very high levels for the foreseeable future and structural deficits are almost equally large. Even if the economy performs in a surprisingly strong and consistent fashion, the budget will be far from balanced. Reducing structural deficits to achieve balance is dependent upon either major entitlement cuts or massive tax increases or some combination of the two. Large upward revenue adjustments, however, may prove difficult to implement.

The Revenue "Ceiling"

Unlike spending, which has outpaced economic growth for the past three decades, revenue levels have been relatively stable (table 37). Even with the Reagan tax cuts, revenues during the 1980s remained remarkably close to prior levels. Since the beginning of World War II, revenues have exceeded 20 percent of GDP only four times. In fiscal years 1969 and 1981, total budget receipts rose to 20.2 percent of GDP, but dropped quickly thereafter. During World War II, total receipts twice moved above 21 percent of GDP but never reached 22 percent.

The political barriers to high tax levels are well known, and they are complemented by economic policy concerns that rising tax burdens may depress growth and international competitiveness. The political and economic definitions of "permissible" revenue levels have proved surprisingly resistant to change, which complicates enormously the task of raising revenues much above 20 percent of GDP and maintaining them at that level over a long period of time. The nearly $250 billion

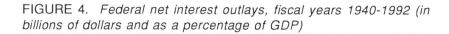

FIGURE 4. *Federal net interest outlays, fiscal years 1940-1992 (in billions of dollars and as a percentage of GDP)*

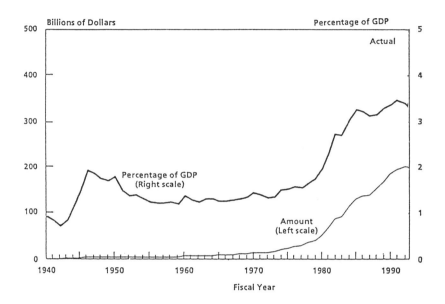

Source: *Federal Debt and Interest Costs* (Washington, DC: Congressional Budget Office, 1993), 3.

in tax increases contained in the Clinton administration's deficit reduction program, for example, will still leave revenues below 20 percent of GDP in FY 1998.[58]

What seems to be, in effect, a revenue "ceiling" means that even greatly reduced discretionary spending levels cannot be supported without large deficits (table 38). Between FY 1993 and FY 2003, projected social security, medicare, and medicaid outlays will rise to over 11 percent under current policy, while net interest outlays are projected at above 3 percent of GDP. If revenue levels remain below 20 percent of GDP, the resources to support other programs, while bringing the budget deficit down, would be extremely meager.

141

TABLE 36. *Baseline and structural deficit projections, fiscal years 1993-2003 (in billions of dollars)*

Fiscal Year	Baseline Deficit	Percent of GDP	Structural Deficit	Percent of GDP
1993	$266	4.3%	$211	3.3%
1994	253	3.9	175	2.6
1995	196	2.9	154	2.2
1996	190	2.6	160	2.2
1997	198	2.6	180	2.3
1998	200	2.5	186	2.3
1999	223	2.7	NA	NA
2000	251	2.9	NA	NA
2001	282	3.1	NA	NA
2002	320	3.3	NA	NA
2003	359	3.6	NA	NA

*Excludes deposit insurance and *Desert Storm* contributions; assumes continuation of discretionary spending caps.
Source: *The Economic and Budget Outlook: An Update* (Washington, DC: Congressional Budget Office, 1993), 25-27.

TABLE 37. *Receipts as a Percentage of GDP, Fiscal Years 1940-1994*

Fiscal Year	Annual Average Percentage of GDP
1940-1944	12.1%
1945-1949	17.8
1950-1954	17.8
1955-1959	17.5
1960-1964	18.2
1965-1969	18.4
1970-1974	18.5
1975-1979	18.5
1980-1984	19.1
1985-1989	18.8
1990-1994 (est.)	18.8

Source: *Supplement, Budget of the United States Government, Fiscal Year 1993, Part Five* (Washington, DC: GPO, 1992), 15-16; *The Economic and Budget Outlook: An Update* (Washington, DC: Congressional Budget Office,1993), 39.

TABLE 38. *The discretionary spending margin, fiscal years 1993-2003 (as percentages of GDP)*

	FY 1993	FY 1998	FY 2003
Retirement and healthcare	8.4%	9.6%	11.2%
Social Security	(4.9)	(4.9)	(5.0)
Medicare	(2.3)	(3.0)	(3.9)
Medicaid	(1.2)	(1.7)	(2.3)
Net interest	3.2	3.2	3.3
Other non-discretionary	3.9	3.3	3.1
Discretionary	8.8	6.9	6.3

Source: *The Economic and Budget Outlook: An Update* (Washington, DC: Congressional Budget Office, 1993), 27.

Preserving other entitlements and discretionary domestic spending at current policy levels would result in continued, large deficits without any defense spending. Cutting these levels in half would bring the budget into balance, but again there would be essentially no room to support defense.

The Budget Policy Dilemma

The spending and deficit dynamics shaping federal budget policy show no signs of weakening, which suggests that the budget outlook for defense will worsen rather than improve. The defense reductions instituted by the Bush and Clinton administrations are substantial in terms of U.S. military capabilities but surprisingly modest when compared to the size of structural deficits and the growth of retirement and healthcare entitlements. With the discretionary spending margin constricting under the combined weight of interest payments and entitlement costs, defense and nondefense programs face the prospect of mounting cutbacks simply to keep deficits at moderately high levels.

The composition of spending policy and chronicity of deficits will also make it extremely difficult to finance a defense buildup should one become necessary. Prior buildups have been funded through deficits and spending cutbacks, but these options cannot be implemented easily or quickly when deficits are already high and most spending is programmed for automatic growth. Because the discretionary portion of the budget is so tightly constrained, the prospects for defense will remain grim for quite some time. It should be emphasized as well that the budget process competition between discretionary defense and nondefense programs is artificial and misleading. The real competition for both is with a few very large and costly entitlements, and this competition is being lost by default.

Notes

1. *An Analysis of the President's February Budgetary Proposals* (Washington, DC: Congressional Budget Office, 1993), II-4.

2. *A Glossary of Terms Used in the Federal Budget Process,* 3d ed. (Washington, DC: Government Accounting Office, 1981), 57.

3. See R. Kent Weaver, "Controlling Entitlements," in *The New Direction in American Politics,* J. E. Chubb and P. E. Peterson, eds. (Washington, DC: Brookings Institution, 1985), 308-11.

4. See Dennis S. Ippolito, "The Budget Process and Budget Policy: Resolving the Mismatch," *Public Administration Review* 52 (January/February 1993): 11.

5. Dennis S. Ippolito, *Uncertain Legacies, Federal Budget Policy from Roosevelt through Reagan* (Charlottesville: University Press of Virginia, 1990), 153.

6. Aaron Wildavsky, *The New Politics of the Budgetary Process* (Glenview, IL: Scott, Foresman, 1988), 346.

7. A few means-tested programs, including subsidized housing and social services grants, are funded through discretionary appropriations. *The Economic and Budget Outlook: Fiscal Years 1994-1998* (Washington, DC: Congressional Budget Office, 1993), 144-45.

8. See Ippolito, *Uncertain Legacies,* 164.

9. Ibid.

10. *Economic and Budget Outlook: Fiscal Years 1994-1998,* 130, 132.

11. On indexing provisions for social welfare programs, see R. Kent Weaver, *Automatic Government, The Politics of Indexation* (Washington, DC: Brookings Institution, 1988).

12. *Congressional Quarterly Almanac, 1976* (Washington, DC: Congressional Quarterly Inc., 1977), 859-60.

13. Ippolito, *Uncertain Legacies,* 179-80.

14. *Fiscal Year 1982 Budget Revisions* (Washington, DC: GPO, 1981), 8.

15. Ibid.

16. Ippolito, *Uncertain Legacies,* 181-85.

17. *Economic and Budget Outlook: Fiscal Years 1994-1998,* 38.

18. Ibid., 48.

19. Ibid., 49.

20. Ippolito, *Uncertain Legacies,* 159-62.

21. For data on trust fund balances, see *Supplement, Budget of the United States Government, Fiscal Year 1993, Part Five* (Washington, DC: GPO, 1992), 173-203.

22. Ippolito, *Uncertain Legacies,* 161.

23. *Congress and the Nation, 1973-1976, Vol. IV* (Washington, DC: Congressional Quarterly Inc., 1977), 407.

24. See Michael J. Boskin, *Too Many Promises: The Uncertain Future of Social Security* (Homewood, IL: Dow Jones-Irvin, 1986), 23-38.

25. *Congress and the Nation, 1977-1980, Vol. V* (Washington, DC: Congressional Quarterly Inc., 1981), 235.

26. Ibid., 236.

27. Ibid. The technical adjustment was designed to correct a flow in the existing benefit formula that overcompensated for inflation.

28. Ippolito, *Uncertain Legacies,* 180.

29. Boskin, 24, 27.

30. Ibid., 35.

31. Ibid., 38.

32. Paul Light, *Artful Work, The Politics of Social Security Reform* (New York: Random House, 1985), 90.

33. *Fiscal Year 1982 Budget Revisions,* 8.

34. Ibid.

35. Ibid.

36. Ibid, 9.

37. *Congress and the Nation, 1981-1984, Vol. VI* (Washington, DC: Congressional Quarterly Inc., 1985), 646.

38. Ibid.

39. Ibid.

40. The retirement age is scheduled to be raised in 6-year stages of 2 months per year ending in 2007 and again in 2027.

41. Joseph A. Pechman, *Federal Tax Policy*, 5th ed. (Washington, DC: Brookings Institution, 1987), 332.

42. The Social Security Amendments of 1983 had included a provision making the OASI and DI trust funds off-budget in 1992. The balanced-budget bills made off-budget status immediate.

43. *Congress and the Nation, Vol. VI,* 521.

44. Henry J. Aaron, *Serious and Unstable Condition, Financing America's Health Care* (Washington, DC: Brookings Institution, 1991), 62.

45. Ippolito, *Uncertain Legacies,* 187-88. The catastrophic illness benefits added to medicare in 1988 were to be entirely financed by beneficiaries, with premiums based on income. The reaction of the elderly against this new medicare surtax was so intense that the program was repealed in 1989.

46. In 1990, the Part B deductible was raised from $75 to $100, the first increase since 1982 and only the third since Part B benefits were established.

47. *Congressional Quarterly Almanac, 1990* (Washington, DC: Congressional Quarterly Inc., 1991), 171.

48. Aaron, 62.

49. *Trends in Health Spending: An Update* (Washington, DC: Congressional Budget Office, 1993), 19.

50. Ibid.

51. Ibid., 20.

52. *The Budget Deficit and Long-Term Economic Growth* (Washington, DC: General Accounting Office, 1992), 3.

53. *The Economic and Budget Outlook: Fiscal Years 1994-1998,* 30. The status of the medicare Part A trust fund is uncertain.

54. Ibid., 31-32.

55. Ibid.

56. James D. Savage, *Balanced Budgets and American Politics* (Ithaca: Cornell University Press, 1988), 1.

57. A recent examination of the economic impact of deficits suggests the dispute is likely to continue: "Do budget deficits matter for the economy or real interest rates in particular? About half the

available empirical studies say yes, and the other half say no. . . . These studies are flawed by an important statistical problem . . . [that] is difficult and is not likely to be resolved soon." Preston J. Miller and William Roberds, "How Little We Know About Deficit Policy Effects," *Federal Reserve Bank of Minneapolis Quarterly Review* 15 (Winter 1992): 2.

58. *An Analysis of the President's February Budgetary Proposals* I-9.

5. Risk, Reversibility, and Defense Planning

WHILE LARGE REDUCTIONS IN the defense budget are inescapable, the scale and timing of these reductions, as well as their effects on the size and shape of the military, remain undetermined. The Clinton administration's 5-year spending plan for defense proposes funding levels of approximately $250 billion annually in budget authority and outlays by the late 1990s, but defense budgets could drop even lower. When completed, the administration's strategic policy review will presumably guide the reshaping of military capabilities, but the "bottom-up" review is already being undercut by funding uncertainties and policy indecisiveness.

The fact that the Clinton administration's defense spending decisions have been decided well in advance of its defense program is not entirely without precedent. Despite the axiom that strategy should shape budgets, defense planners have always had to cope with politically realistic resource constraints when attempting to balance threats and risks against capabilities. In a similar fashion, decisions about roles and missions to guide the training and arming of U.S. forces have rarely, if ever, been divorced from highly politicized conflicts over budgetary allocations.

There are also numerous precedents for subordinating defense needs to nondefense budgetary requirements. Political demands to boost domestic spending helped to drive down defense budgets after World War II and, to a lesser extent, after Vietnam. Defense budget ceilings have also been employed in order to control deficits. The distinctive problem posed today is that the administration is misrepresenting the "peace dividend" controversy, thereby undermining its ability to protect what could already be substantially underfunded defense budgets against mounting congressional cuts.

Furthermore, the Clinton administration and Congress have

insured that funding uncertainties will endure by avoiding resolute action to control entitlement spending and to reduce structural deficits. The funding constraints on discretionary programs, especially defense, are tightening, with no prospects for any relief over at least the next decade. Because the defense budget's fiscal vulnerabilities are magnified by its political weaknesses, policymakers will almost certainly find themselves forced to accept heightened risks as budgets fall behind planning levels, and, as risks mount, it will become harder and harder to reverse course. The simple fact is that defense planners are facing a series of budgetary shocks whose dimensions are either not well understood or are not being acknowledged by political leaders.

The Peace Dividend

The Clinton administration's FY 1994 defense budget was presented as "the first truly post-Cold War budget."[1] This rhetoric has encouraged the mistaken perception that substantial savings from the end of the Cold War have yet to be realized. What is more, for members of Congress who hold this perception, the Clinton defense cuts do not go nearly far enough. House Armed Services Committee chairman Dellums, for example, has sharply attacked the Clinton budget for its alleged timidity, arguing that "There would be a significant cost to delaying for another year our inevitable adjustment to the post-Cold War world."[2] Dellums has urged that defense be cut more rapidly and more deeply than Clinton has proposed, stating, "The sooner the end point for the reduction in force structure can be established, the smoother, cheaper, and better the transition will be."[3]

With total discretionary spending subject to annual spending limits, defense cuts are the only source for additional domestic program support. For Dellums and others in Congress, the defense budget represents, among other things, a potential funding windfall for domestic programs. This approach to the defense budget ignores recent defense spending trends and grossly underestimates the impact that precipitous future cuts will have on military capabilities.

Cold War Spending

The defense spending levels of the past few years are not Cold War budgets. When Ronald Reagan left office, he submitted a 5-year defense spending plan still geared toward the Soviet threat. The last Department of Defense analysis of Soviet military power issued during Reagan's tenure stated that "Soviet goals . . . are unchanged. . . . It would be a mistake . . . to regard political and military shifts as mirroring fundamental changes in the nature of the Soviet regime."[4] The post-Reagan defense budget prescription accordingly called for sharply increased spending "to continue modernization of U.S. strategic and conventional forces, maintain readiness, and improve combat sustainability."[5]

While the Reagan administration's position no doubt defined the upper limit of Cold War defense funding, comparisons with recent budgets are still quite striking (table 39). For fiscal years 1993 and 1994, total budget authority requests submitted by the Bush and Clinton administrations are nearly $200 billion below Reagan's Cold War budgets, and outlay differences are more than $125 billion. The defense budget shares under the Bush and Clinton programs are not only well below Reagan's but represent the lowest since the New Deal.

Of course, the Reagan defense buildup was neither as massive nor as injurious to domestic spending as domestic program advocates critics have alleged. Real defense spending growth was halted by Congress during Reagan's second term, and neither the defense budget share nor GNP share ever came close to Reagan's initial budget program.[6] Defense outlays rose by nearly $170 billion between fiscal years 1980 and 1990, but domestic outlays (entitlements and discretionary programs) increased by $330 billion.

By the end of Reagan's tenure, on the eve of the Cold War's demise, the three-decades-long decline in the relative level of defense spending was still in place. As Weidenbaum stated, "The overall pattern is clear: the economic impact of defense activities peaked decades ago and has been declining, albeit irregularly, ever since."[7] The peace dividend claims after Vietnam failed to take into account actual defense and domestic spending trends during the war, and the post-Cold War claims suffer from an even greater distortion.

TABLE 39. *The Reagan administration's Cold War defense plan, fiscal years 1990-1994 (in billions of dollars)*

Fiscal Year	Budget Authority	Outlays	Percent of Total Outlays
1990	$315.2	$303.0	26.3%
1991	330.8	314.4	26.0
1992	346.1	326.4	26.2
1993 (Reagan)	361.4	339.9	26.6
(Bush)	281.0	291.3	19.2
1994 (Reagan)	376.6	354.3	27.0
(Clinton)	263.4	276.9	18.3

Source: *Budget of the United States Government, Fiscal Year 1990* (Washington, DC: GPO, 1989), 2-17; *Budget of the United States Government, Fiscal Year 1993, Supplement, Part Five*, (Washington, DC: GPO, 1992), 42, 69; *Budget of the United States Government, Fiscal Year 1994, Appendix* (Washington, DC: GPO, 1993), 6.

Measuring the Peace Dividend

An accurate assessment of the Cold War peace dividend depends upon plausible assumptions about what would have occurred to the defense budget if the Soviet threat had not disappeared. If Cold War funding is defined as the continuation of FY 1990 real spending levels, then the Bush administration's post-Cold War base force plan represented over $540 billion in cumulative savings through FY 1997 (figure 5).   A less generous Cold War defense budget, with moderately declining real spending, yields a smaller but still sizable base force peace dividend.

Perhaps the most relevant comparison, however, is between the estimated base force savings and the $275 billion and $250 billion FY 1997 alternative paths. The $275 billion path, which is roughly equivalent to the Force C option proposed by former Secretary of Defense Aspin in 1992, increases the peace

FIGURE 5. *Peace dividend estimates, defense discretionary budget authority, fiscal years 1989-1997* (in billions of dollars)*

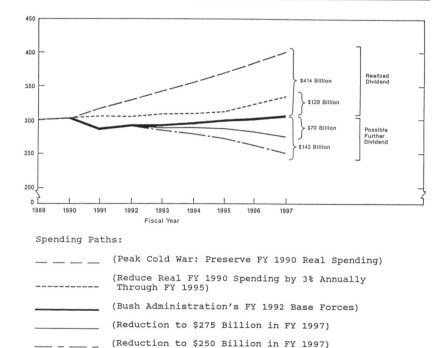

Spending Paths:

_ _ _ _ (Peak Cold War: Preserve FY 1990 Real Spending)

---------- (Reduce Real FY 1990 Spending by 3% Annually Through FY 1995)

▬▬▬▬▬ (Bush Administration's FY 1992 Base Forces)

_____ (Reduction to $275 Billion in FY 1997)

_ _ _ _ (Reduction to $250 Billion in FY 1997)

*Excludes budget authority for Operation *Desert Shield* and *Desert Storm.* Source: *The Economic and Budget Outlook: Fiscal Years 1993-1997* (Washington, DC: Congressional Budget Office, 1992), 53.

dividend by $70 billion above the base force savings. The $250 billion path, which is equivalent to the Clinton administration's defense spending plan, more than doubles this additional dividend, and its $140+ billion in cumulative defense savings cushions domestic programs against real spending cutbacks.

The dimensions of the pre-Clinton peace dividend are equally impressive in terms of force level reductions. During the Reagan buildup, the active-duty personnel peak was 2.174 million, reached in FY 1987.[8]   In FY 1990, the major components of force structure were close to the peak levels of the Reagan years, with a total military force strength of 3.3 million.   Under the Bush, Aspin, and Clinton post-Cold War plans, the projected reductions from these peaks are substantial (table 40).   The Bush base force program would have cut the number of army divisions by more than one-third and the number of air force fighter wings by more than one-fourth. The 1992 Aspin Force C proposal included deeper cuts but still would have required an estimated $275 billion in FY 1997 funding. The Clinton defense program has the lowest FY 1997 cost and will necessitate additional force level cuts when compared to the base force or to Force C.

A very large peace dividend, whether measured in dollars or forces, had been integrated into defense planning levels well before President Clinton took office. The new cuts by the Clinton administration are not by any means coming out of Cold War defense budgets. Instead, additional defense cuts are being imposed on an already steep defense decline, in order to expand funding for domestic program initiatives. By failing to acknowledge the magnitude of the realized peace dividend, the administration may find itself encouraging Congress to extend defense savings well beyond what Clinton defense officials believe to be prudent.

Another facet of the peace dividend debate that is being ignored or distorted is the recent history of domestic spending trends. While discretionary domestic outlays increased only modestly during the Reagan presidency, particularly in comparison to defense or entitlements, growth rates over the past several years have been quite high (table 41). Since FY

TABLE 40. *Force reductions under alternative defense programs*

	Cold War Force (FY 1990)	FY 1997 Projections		
		Base Force	Aspin Force C	FY 1994 Budget
Active duty personnel (in millions)	2.1	1.6	1.4	1.4
Guard and Reserve (in millions)	1.2	0.9	0.9	NA
Army divisions*	28	18	15	15
Air Force fighter wings*	36	26	18	20
Major warships*	545	450	340	NA
Projected FY 1997 cost (budget authority, in billions)	$400	$291	$270	$248

*Active and reserve (The FY 1994 Army strength includes 10 active divisions and 15 reserve brigades).

Source: The Cold War force levels are from *Report of the Secretary of Defense to the President and the Congress, January 1991* (Washington, DC: GPO, 1991), 113-16; the Cold War FY 1997 budget authority estimate is from *The Economic and Budget Outlook: Fiscal Years 1993-1997* (Washington, DC: Congressional Budget Office, 1992), 53; data for the Base Force and Force C options are from Congress, House, Committee on the Budget, *Hearing, National Defense Funding and the Fiscal Year 1993 Budget* (Washington, DC: GPO, 1992), 45-48; the Clinton administration data are from *An Analysis of the President's February Budgetary Proposals* (Washington, DC: Congressional Budget Office, 1993), IV-2, IV-7, and *The New York Times,* September 2, 1993, A9.

TABLE 41. *Outlay growth for major spending categories, fiscal years 1980-1994 (annual percentage increase)*

Fiscal Year	Discretionary Domestic	Defense	Entitlements and Mandatory
1980	13.1%	15.2%	17.4%
1981	5.7	17.9	16.8
1982	-6.7	17.6	9.4
1983	2.0	12.9	10.4
1984	4.1	9.0	-1.3
1985	7.7	11.0	10.7
1986	1.2	8.2	2.1
1987	0.0	3.2	2.3
1988	7.6	3.0	5.1
1989	6.7	4.5	6.5
1990	8.0	-1.2	7.8
1991	7.1	6.5	11.8
1992	9.5	-4.8	12.1
1993	8.5	0.0	8.3
1994 (est.)	4.7	-8.9	6.0

Source: *The Economic and Budget Outlook: Fiscal Years 1994-1998* (Washington, DC: Congressional Budget Office, 1993), 44, 130.

1988, the average annual outlay increase for discretionary domestic programs has been nearly 7.5 percent, which is only slightly below the rate of growth in entitlement spending. The discretionary spending cutbacks of the past several years have been entirely absorbed by the defense budget, while domestic programs have been allowed to grow.

In addition, the distinction between discretionary domestic programs and entitlements is simply that the former are funded by annual appropriations. Both categories comprise programs which are "domestic" in nature, and an accurate measure of domestic spending, particularly in the context of budget priorities, properly would include all discretionary and entitlement programs that serve domestic purposes. By this measure, the domestic program share of the federal budget is extremely high (approximately 65 percent) and continuing to increase while the defense share, now approximately 20 percent, will be at pre-World War II levels by the mid-1990s.

The legitimacy of peace dividend claims ultimately rests upon defense spending's having "crowded out" domestic programs. During World War II, when defense accounted for almost 90 percent of the federal budget, domestic programs obviously could not be funded at prewar levels. During the Korean War, when the defense budget peaked at nearly 70 percent of total spending, nondefense spending again declined from prewar levels. The Vietnam and especially the post-Cold War spending patterns are quite different. The domestic sector expanded during Vietnam and again during the defense buildup of the 1980s. In both instances, there is no real basis for inflated peace dividends. Nevertheless, the defense budget remains exposed to domestic transfer pressures, because neither the Bush nor the Clinton administration has challenged these spurious claims.

Risk and Deterrence

While U.S. defense strategy is still very much in transition, there is a consensus among policymakers that substantial military capabilities must be maintained indefinitely. The dissolution of the Soviet Union has removed the greatest threat to U.S. interests, and, as a consequence, the United States no longer needs the military capabilities to fight a global war. The United States continues to face other threats against which military forces might be required, including regional conflicts, nuclear weapons proliferation, and terrorism and drug trafficking. It is also probable that the United States will play a leading role in international peacekeeping and humanitarian assistance operations. The military capabilities defined by these contingencies will permit forces to be reduced well below Cold War levels, with the mix of forces adjusted accordingly.

The existing policy consensus extends to forward deployments of U.S. forces to support its system of alliances. The NATO commitment is an enduring one, buttressed by land and naval deployments. In the past, the United States has depended on forward deployments in Asia, and ground troops are likely to remain in Japan and South Korea for the foreseeable future. Here again, the force levels will generally be well below those maintained during the Cold War.

Budgetary Support

If some general parameters of defense planning are clear, there remain deep disagreements about the levels of budgetary support needed for a ready and capable mix of forces. Part of the problem is that reduced forces may not prove to be proportionately cheaper. As one analyst has emphasized, "The much smaller high-tech military of the post-Cold War era requires a Cold War budget to keep it running."[9] The potential effectiveness of the force presently being planned will be heavily dependent on upgraded airlift and sealift capabilities and on technologically advanced equipment. With a substantial portion of the military's current stock of weaponry scheduled for replacement before the end of this decade, the fiscal repercussions of advanced weaponry cannot be avoided for very long.[10]

The Clinton administration therefore faces a host of difficult weapons acquisition choices, including successor generations of fighter and attack aircraft, tanks and armored vehicles, helicopters, and submarines to modernize U.S. forces. The Bush administration had already instituted sharp procurement reductions by the time it left office, terminating purchases of weapons systems such as the Abrams tank, Apache helicopter, the F-15 aircraft, and the Peacekeeper (MX) missile and Trident submarine.[11] The 1993 procurement budget canceled plans for purchasing next-generation tactical and stealth aircraft, capped the B-2 bomber program at 15 percent of the originally planned level of 132, and canceled or deferred other high-profile modernization programs.[12] The Bush administration planned to hold down modernization costs by emphasizing development, rather than production, of new weapons systems. As a result of these and related efforts, the real cuts in weapons programs during the 1990-1993 period were about twice those for personnel and operating costs.[13]

Still, the Bush administration would eventually have had to choose between smaller forces or less modern forces, since the weapons programs to which it was committed probably could not have been accommodated within its budgets.[14] The Clinton administration may soon face the same choice, since it proposes to cut weapons acquisition costs by more than $35 billion below the final Bush budget over the FY 1994-1998 period, with $15 billion of this reduction in research, development, test, and evaluation (RDT&E).[15] In addition, the Clinton weapons acquisition budgets contain no allowance for underfunding in its predecessor's budgets and rely heavily on unrealized and unspecified management efficiencies.[16]

The extremely tight investment budgets for the next several years pose a serious dilemma. The Clinton administration has argued that its smaller force will be comparable in capabilities and effectiveness to a larger force because of superior mobility and technologically advanced equipment. With procurement and RDT&E funding being reduced significantly, it will be very difficult to provide the advanced weaponry for this force without extremely prescient selectivity. In the past, less demanding standards of selectivity have been hard to meet because of congressional intervention and the inherent difficulty of predicting weapons development and production costs.

Should the administration receive all that it requests for defense, it still must overcome the political and practical complexities of the weapons acquisition process. More probable is that Congress will not fully fund the Clinton budgets, compounding the problems on the investment side of the defense budget and forcing policymakers to choose between force levels and weapons programs. From a budgetary perspective, the attraction of reduced force levels lies in the immediate savings produced by fast-spending accounts, such as personnel and operations and maintenance.

Force Levels

The issue of force size reduction is crucial in terms of capabilities and also in terms of the morale and quality of military personnel. The latter considerations are particularly relevant for an all-volunteer force, since the military must be able to reduce force size without inordinate sacrifices in skills, experience, and commitment. The projected cutbacks in force levels under the base force were enormous—nearly 550,000 active duty personnel, along with 231,000 reservists and 229,000 civilians.[17] By phasing in these reductions over 5 years, base force program planners hoped to minimize involuntary separations and to ease the transition to a civilian economy for those who left the service. Bringing down the force faster and further, however, cannot be accomplished without large numbers of forced separations, which raises the specter of shattered morale for those who remain. General Powell recently warned that it is possible to "break the force" by arbitrarily forcing out those who had been asked to make the military a career:

> You start to break faith with the troops, you start to break the legal contract but more than that, the informal, implicit contract of faith that exists between leaders of the Armed Forces and people of our great country and the young men and women who have decided to serve.
> If after winning [Desert Storm] and winning the Cold War . . . all the members of the Armed Forces see nothing but a feeding frenzy up in the Congress for the purpose of cutting the budget . . . they will all start to feel that that contract of faith has been broken.[18]

Continually stepped-up force reduction schedules pose

unmistakable problems in force structure planning and in readiness. These problems are intensified when there is pervasive uncertainty about the final force size, the mix between active and reserve forces, and the balance between forces and capabilities.

Force Readiness

Additional pressure on personnel accounts results from the lag in realized savings from operations and maintenance (O&M) accounts and family housing accounts. O&M accounts, which comprise about 30 percent of defense spending, cannot be drawn down uniformly as personnel levels are reduced.[19] Certain O&M costs are fixed for the short term, and projected savings from base closings and consolidations may materialize only over an extended period of time.[20]

The O&M accounts that can produce more immediate savings are those that directly affect training and maintenance, and disproportionate reductions here would be extremely controversial. One of the most serious weaknesses plaguing the military during the 1970s was inadequate readiness. Budget cuts had resulted in what critics called a "hollow force"—units that were undermanned, underequipped, and undertrained.[21] The Reagan administration's defense buildup highlighted the necessity for upgrading readiness and training, and the measurable gains during the 1980s were impressive.[22] In addition, the performance of U.S. military units during the Operation *Desert Shield/Desert Storm* deployments has greatly buttressed the arguments for very high readiness standards.

Many O&M accounts, then, are inviting targets for budget-cutting efforts, because they are fast-spending accounts. At the same time, these accounts directly affect the quality and balance of U.S. forces. If the smaller U.S. forces of the future are to take advantage of increasingly advanced weaponry, the necessary investments in readiness and training seem likely to push up O&M costs. Indeed, the rapid response, highly mobile forces designed to meet post-Cold War contingencies and threats must be highly flexible, which presumably will entail an even greater emphasis on readiness and training.

161

The possibility of a serious degradation in force readiness is sufficiently troubling that former Secretary of Defense Aspin established a Readiness Task Force to monitor readiness and to provide an "early-warning system" for defense planners.[23] While readiness problems are generally viewed as a long-term concern rather than an immediate danger, even moderate funding shortages could have adverse short-term effects. As Aspin's successor, William J. Perry, has conceded, "It would not take much of a decrement to require the Army to curtail its maneuvers, the Navy to keep ships in port, and the Air Force to reduce flying hours."[24] Sen. John McCain, who has been at the center of the readiness debate, argues that the impact of reduced funding is already being felt. "In spite of the efforts of our services," states McCain, "we are going hollow. We are losing the combat readiness and edge that is an essential aspect of deterrence, defense and the ability to deter aggression."[25]

With budgets continuing to decline, forced tradeoffs between force size and readiness appear inevitable, particularly if the U.S. does not develop clear standards for committing its forces in "contingency operations." The unanticipated but substantial new mission requirements that the Clinton administration imposed on the military during 1993, for example, were not compensated for by budgetary adjustments. Instead, funding for these peacekeeping and humanitarian operations was drawn from existing O&M accounts. If similar types of contingency operations are mounted in the future without corresponding budgetary adjustments, readiness problems will simply be exacerbated.

Force Capabilities

The prospect that major tradeoffs between force size and procurement or O&M will be necessary to meet budget ceilings is even more troublesome given the arguable capabilities of a 1.4 million active-duty force. The centerpiece of mainstream defense planning is the *Desert Storm* equivalent, which involves the capability for fighting a major regional war, but there is considerable disagreement about the forces necessary to fight and to win against an Iraq equivalent foe. While Secretary of Defense Aspin claimed that certain elements of the force that defeated Iraq could be eliminated in defining what he termed the "force that matters," Aspin's measure has been sharply criticized by military experts for ignoring "technology, terrain, location, leadership, coalitions, and the introduction of nuclear or other nonconventional weapons" and for reducing arbitrarily force size.[26]

The criticism of Aspin's methodology is even more pointed when multiple contingencies are considered. The Force C option, which was Aspin's stated preference, included an extended *Desert Storm* capability, along with capabilities for fighting simultaneously another major regional contingency, for meeting a Panama-sized contingency, and for mounting a substantial humanitarian relief effort. The base force, which provided these same capabilities, assumed much higher force level requirements, including three more active Army divisions, 110 more ships, five more active fighter wings, and a larger Marine component.[27] The base force's larger size allowed for a substantial forward presence in Europe and elsewhere to supply deterrence and strategic depth.

The base force program was deliberately conservative in terms of risk. Force planning was geared to a variety of contingencies and to continual uncertainty about the nature of future threats. Forward presence was an important, indeed indispensable, part of deterrence.[28] Force size was generous, calculated to achieve decisive victories when force was employed and to maintain a strategic reserve to meet simultaneous contingencies.

Options for a smaller force currently being considered obviously involve higher risk, since the margins for allowable error in force planning are greatly reduced. The Force C option, which attempts to minimize future risk, cannot be funded at planned budget levels. There is a strong possibility, under current budget limits, that force size will have to be reduced well below 1.4 million active-duty personnel simply in order to accommodate acceptable levels of modernization and readiness. If Congress decides to cut defense budgets even further, the force size problem will be more acute, and the concomitant erosion in military capabilities will be more serious.

Reconstitution and Reversibility

In addition to the immediate capabilities of U.S. Forces, defense planning must take into account the possibility of major buildups if U.S. security is seriously threatened. The reconstitution capability of U.S. forces involves both military manpower and the defense industrial base needed to support upgraded forces. While post-Cold War defense budgets cannot support forces or an industrial base at wartime levels, there has to be sufficient funding to permit a reasonably rapid buildup.

Manpower and Mobilization

The total force concept, which serves as the basis for reconstituting forces, includes active-duty personnel and reserve forces.[29] The latter includes selected reserves (peacetime training and military unit assignments), individual ready reserves (military experience but no peacetime training), and retired reserves. While all reserve categories could conceivably supply personnel during a major war, the selected reserves are by far the most important component of reserve force planning.

There are currently about 1.1 million selected reserves out of the more than three million total reserve personnel.[30] The reliance on selected reserves differs greatly among the services.[31] The Army has approximately one-half of its overall strength in reserves and accounts for two-thirds of reserve personnel in all the services. The Air Force has nearly 30 percent of its combined force in reserve units. The Navy and Marine Corps reserve levels are about 20 percent.

The use of reserve forces in wartime is a long-standing tradition in the U.S. and in many other countries. Indeed, reliance on reserves is considerably higher in most of the NATO countries than in the U.S. For NATO countries excluding the U.S., the reserve share of total manning was 64 percent at the end of 1991, compared to 46 percent for the U.S.[32] Further, the NATO allies are moving toward an even greater reliance on reserve forces, as active-duty strength levels are being sharply reduced, while reserve strength levels are being kept fairly stable.[33]

The United States has higher readiness needs and more extensive and geographically dispersed military commitments than do its NATO allies, but it shares the need for cutting defense costs. Since reserve units are less costly to operate during peacetime than are active units, there is strong support in Congress for increasing the reliance on selected reserves and for employing new and even less costly types of reserve units. The latter include cadre units for ground forces, nested ships, and teamed air squadrons and stored air wings, all of which would be manned at low peacetime levels with mixed active and reserve personnel.[34]

The cost differential between selected reserve and active units can be substantial. A reserve ground combat unit can be operated at approximately one-fourth the cost of an active unit.[35] Reserve air unit savings can be 30-40 percent below active unit costs, and reserve ship savings can be as high as 20 percent.[36] The proposed new types of reserve units may yield even greater savings. A cadre division with 25 percent of the active personnel needed to man the unit normally has an estimated cost of approximately 70 percent of a selected reserve unit.[37]

While the budgetary attraction of increased reliance on the reserves is obvious, there are potential drawbacks to significantly altering the balance between active and reserve forces. Active units can generally be mobilized and prepared for war far more quickly than reserve units, although there is a good deal of controversy about the amount of additional time required to make reserve units available for combat. The Army estimates that substantial training time is required to bring reserve units, particularly ground combat units, to required combat readiness levels (table 42). Navy and Air Force reserve units, by comparison, are viewed as highly ready, although the two services used their reserves very differently during the Persian Gulf War. The Marine Corps, which used reserve combat units early and extensively in the war with Iraq, has reported that readiness levels between reserve and active units were not appreciably different.[38]

The seriousness of readiness delays depends on the types of conflicts fought by U.S. forces. In the case of a major war, most analysts agree that there would be sufficient time to mobilize and train reserve units and even to reintroduce conscription to supplement active and reserve forces, provided that political leaders respond quickly to the evolving threat. For large-scale regional wars, such as the Persian Gulf War, warning times may be short or nonexistent, and readiness delays would be much more serious.

TABLE 42. *Training times to bring selected reserve units to combat readiness*

Army	Roundout Brigade	1 to 3 months longer than active Army divisions
	Division	2 months to a year longer than active Army divisions
Navy	Ships	About equal to nondeployed active ships
Air Force	Fighter Squadron	About equal to Continental U.S.-based active units (2 weeks)

Source: *Structuring U.S. Forces After the Cold War: Costs and Effects of Increased Reliance on the Reserves* (Washington, DC: Congressional Budget Office, 1992), 19.

If regional wars of relatively limited duration define the primary capabilities for which future military forces are being planned, then the potential utility of reserve forces, particularly for ground combat, is considerably reduced. It would also make little sense to call up reserve forces for short-term contingencies, such as humanitarian and peacekeeping operations, that represent supplementary planning capabilities for U.S. forces. Of course, these limitations would be even greater for the newer types of reserve units being proposed than for selected reserve units.

As with so many aspects of defense policy planning, however, the manpower issue may ultimately be decided upon the basis of cost-associated factors, rather than military capabilities. Moreover, Congress refused to support the Bush administration's request to reduce reserve forces in proportion to active forces. The projected active-duty personnel level in the Clinton defense program is linked to reserve force reductions even larger than those proposed by the Bush administration.[39] Unless Congress reverses course, or increases defense budgets, the 1.4 million active-duty force may be unattainable.

Defense Industrial Base

The defense industrial base must be able to supply equipment and weaponry to a smaller post-Cold War force and should possess a reconstitution capability to expand production quickly and significantly if necessary. The defense industrial base has the responsibility of maintaining U.S. leadership in technology development for current and future weaponry. In the past, defense budgets have been large enough to support production capacity for a wide variety of weapons and to fund research and development programs for new weapons systems, but rapidly diminishing investment budgets may adversely affect production capacity and technology development.

Even without these imminent funding difficulties, the defense industrial base would be facing major challenges. The "quasi-arsenal" system upon which the U.S. depended during the Cold War has been shrinking for quite some time, as the federal government has largely abandoned equipping, operating, and owning defense plants.[40] The number of companies whose sole or primary business is defense-related has been decreasing, and there has been a parallel shrinkage in the overall American manufacturing base.

The abrupt downturn in budgetary support for weapons programs may already be discouraging defense companies

167

from undertaking the long-term investments necessary to develop new technologies. In addition, as major contractors are forced to reduce their production capabilities, it becomes more and more difficult to maintain the supporting networks of subcontractors and of energy, telecommunications, and transportation infrastructure systems.[41] Thus, the capabilities necessary "for a surge and expansion capacity in the event of emergency" may become seriously attenuated.[42]

The contraction of the defense industrial base will not have a uniform impact on the estimated 420 industries that constitute the defense industrial base, since many of these industries are not heavily dependent on defense production.[43] There are, however, a number of critical industrial sectors whose dependence on defense sales is very high. In 1990, for example, 12 industrial groupings had a defense share of total output that ranged from approximately one-quarter (ammunition; aircraft and missile equipment) to virtually 100 percent (shipbuilding and repair; tank and tank components).[44] These industries have absorbed significant losses in sales and in employment as a result of budget authority reductions over the past several years, and their losses will probably mount as a result of the ongoing decline in defense-related economic activity. For some industries, such as tanks and submarines, there is the possibility that even minimal production capabilities might eventually be lost.

Given the recognized importance of maintaining an adequate industrial base, defense experts are considering ways to cushion defense firms from the full impact of an ongoing budgetary contraction. Among the proposals receiving serious attention are those for dual-use technologies, which would allow defense firms to switch between civilian and defense goods; developing to prototype, which would require funding only for development costs until weapons are actually needed; skilled worker training programs; more flexible and less burdensome military specifications requirements and defense acquisition regulations; and fully funded research and development programs.[45] Most defense policy analysts also agree that the federal government must improve its often adversarial relationships with defense industries in a manner that will provide financial safeguards without subjecting defense industries to arbitrary regulations and unfounded criticisms.[46]

While some of these proposals might prove useful, the funding uncertainties facing defense firms will complicate enormously the task of maintaining an adequate expansion capability. There is a crucial difference between predictably reduced defense budgets and unpredictably reduced defense budgets. With even quite optimistic defense spending levels in place over the next several years, it will be difficult to balance force structure, readiness, and modernization, much less to fund an ongoing expansion capability for the defense industry. With defense spending at even lower levels, which is considerably more likely, the margin for supporting future industrial base capabilities will be close to nonexistent.

Reversibility

The technical planning problems for reconstituting forces and defense industrial production are formidable under any circumstances. It is also worth noting that political leadership has, in the past, responded slowly and reluctantly to evolving threats, and the notion that somehow future national security planning will be distinctively more perceptive and determined is probably fanciful. It is entirely possible, then, that future military buildups, like past ones, will occur only after unanticipated crises or abrupt reversals in judgments about U.S. interests and threats to those interests.

Moreover, future buildups must overcome fiscal as well as political obstacles. Reversing federal spending policy to accommodate a sharp increase in defense is becoming progressively more difficult, given the overwhelming size and automatic growth of the nondefense portion of the budget. With extremely high deficit and debt levels in place, debt-financed defense buildups are similarly circumscribed. The funding options employed during World War II, the Korean and Vietnam Wars, and the 1980s defense buildup have been severely curtailed and cannot be restored without protracted, painful adjustments in nondefense budget policies.

The budgetary squeeze on defense therefore combines two undesirable outcomes. Because defense budgets are extremely tight, greater risk will have to be accepted in decisions about force structure, readiness, and modernization. Because nondefense budget policies are so constraining, reversibility in defense spending will be extremely limited. If potential reversibility were easier, then higher risk might be more tolerable. As it stands, there is the daunting prospect of high risk and low reversibility.

The Quest for Balance

The difficulties faced by the United States in balancing defense needs against competing budgetary demands are shared by many of its allies. The British Defense Ministry has announced that by 1996, defense spending will be reduced to a 50-year low of 3.2 percent of GDP, and defense ministry officials are resisting even deeper cuts sought by the Treasury Ministry.[47] NATO officials are seeking to establish new force requirements that will arrest what General John M. Shalikashvili, chairman of the Joint Chiefs of Staff and former NATO supreme commander, describes as "a kind of free fall of forces" taking place in some nations.[48] Contrary to a 1991 NATO agreement to reduce post-Cold War active forces by 25 percent, Belgium has reduced its forces by 60 percent and, Germany, Britain, and the Netherlands by 50 percent.[49] NATO military leaders are implementing a smaller force structure and lower readiness levels than recently had been agreed to even as risks and threats are being reexamined in order to determine new force requirements. For the NATO countries, as for the U.S., the rush to cut defense is being fueled by distortions in nondefense spending policies.

The industrialized democracies have spending-control problems that mirror the retirement and healthcare entitlement quandary in the United States.[50] There has been a common drift toward the universalization of benefit programs, and the fiscal repercussions of this drift have been amplified by aging populations and low economic growth. As costs have risen far more rapidly than anticipated, a number of countries have found, as has the United States, that it is politically easier, but fiscally less advantageous, to cut benefits for low-income groups than for middle-class beneficiaries.[51]

As a consequence, major retrenchments in the scope and spending of the welfare state will eventually be necessary, and this will necessitate greatly reduced subsidies to the growing proportion of the population that is above the traditional retirement age. In practical terms, reduced subsidies translate into higher retirement ages, less generous indexing of benefits, healthcare service restrictions, and either direct means-testing or indirect (taxation of benefits received) means-testing for individual benefits.[52] In effect, the industrialized democracies must "modernize the welfare state," by taking into account the very different "demographic, labor-market, family-household, and economic conditions" that exist today, as opposed to the societal frameworks for which welfare systems were initially designed.[53] Reform and retrenchment appear inevitable, given the widely recognized imperatives of controlling budgets and stimulating economic growth.

Inevitable does not mean soon, of course, and this poses a unique dilemma for the United States. By the time that political leaders in the United States finally enter the thicket of welfare state modernization, defense will have been forced down to levels that may be grossly inadequate for a global superpower, and the pace of the defense build-down may have exacted a heavy price in terms of the quality, readiness, and capabilities of U.S. forces. Further, by the time that entitlement retrenchments begin to yield appreciable savings, defense budgets will have been even more severely strained.

For the United States, establishing a reasonable balance between defense and nondefense needs depends upon a realistic understanding of budget policy. It is absolutely clear that the past investment in defense served the U.S. well in winning the Cold War, and this investment neither starved domestic needs nor created enduring deficit problems. It is equally clear that even very severe cutbacks in future defense levels will have only a modest impact on structural deficit problems. Therefore, as one assesses the almost casual abandonment of the base force and its replacement by an undefined but less-costly alternative, it is difficult to resist the conclusion that the United States is trading off important and enduring military capabilities for ephemeral short-term savings.

From a national security perspective, there would be considerably less risk in stabilizing defense budgets over the next several years, than in pursuing the current course of undefined budget contraction. Stabilization would yield savings but would allow force levels to be reduced gradually, while permitting defense planners to reconfigure force structure in response to actual changes in the international environment. If, by the late 1990s, real and potential threats have diminished, additional force reductions could be implemented, again with force levels and drawdowns being determined by strategic requirements.

It is useful to recall that during the 1920s, when budgets were balanced and spending actually declined from year to year, defense accounted for about one-fifth of federal outlays.[54] In the mid-1930s, as domestic program needs expanded and budget deficits grew, defense dropped to about 10 percent of federal spending.[55] As late as 1940, when the security threats against the U.S. from Germany and Japan were undeniably serious, defense was 1.7 percent of GNP and 17.5 percent of the total budget.[56] It then took 3 years to build U.S. forces to peak levels.

It was difficult to reverse the defense decline before World War II, and it will undoubtedly be even harder to do so in the years to come. The presidential commitment and strategic consensus that protected defense against competing budgetary needs during most of the Cold War era have largely dissipated. Whether they will be reestablished in sufficient time to redefine and protect defense needs in the future remains to be seen. What is quite evident at this point, however, is that nondefense spending and deficit challenges of unprecedented magnitude must be overcome if the balance between strategic requirements and defense budget commitments is to be restored.

172

Notes

1. *National Journal* 25 (April 3, 1993): 823.

2. *National Journal* 25 (May 22, 1993): 1222.

3. *Defense News*, August 2-8, 1993, 17.

4. *Soviet Military Power: An Assessment of the Threat 1988* (Washington, DC: Department of Defense, 1988), 7.

5. *Budget of the United States Government, Fiscal Year 1990* (Washington, DC: GPO, 1989), 2-17.

6. The initial Reagan budget program called for defense outlays to climb from 23 percent in FY 1980 to 37.6 percent in FY 1986 and from 5.2 percent to 7.0 percent of GNP over the same period. *Fiscal Year 1982 Budget Revisions* (Washington, DC: GPO, 1981), 13, 124-25.

7. Murray Weidenbaum, *Small Wars, Big Defense* (New York: Oxford University Press, 1992), 112.

8. *Annual Report to the Congress, Fiscal Year 1990, Frank C. Carlucci, Secretary of Defense* (Washington, DC: GPO, 1989), 226.

9. Franklin C. Spinney, *Defense Power Games* (Washington, DC: Fund for Constitutional Government, 1990), quoted in *National Journal* 23 (April 13, 1991): 889.

10. Ibid.

11. *An Analysis of the President's Budgetary Proposals for Fiscal Year 1993* (Washington, DC: Congressional Budget Office, 1992), 68.

12. Ibid.

13. *An Analysis of the President's February Budgetary Proposals* (Washington, DC: Congressional Budget Office, 1993), IV-9.

14. Ibid., IV-8-9.

15. Ibid., IV-6.

16. Ibid., IV-8-9.

17. Congress, Senate, Committee on Armed Services, *Hearings, Threat Assessment, Military Strategy, and Defense Planning* (Washington, DC: GPO, 1992), 490.

18. Ibid., 514.

19. These accounts include payments for the following: (1) fuel; (2) repair and maintenance of weapons; (3) medical care, housing, food, and other support services for military personnel; (4) maintenance and operation of bases in U.S. and abroad; and (5) salaries for most civilians employed by the Department of Defense. *An Analysis of the President's Budgetary Proposals for Fiscal Year 1993*, 65-66.

20. Ibid., 67. The costs of closing bases are usually included in the military construction budget, but the O&M accounts will eventually realize the recurring savings.

21. For a discussion of some of the quantitative measures that are used to measure readiness, see *Annual Report to the Congress, Fiscal Year 1987, Caspar W. Weinberger, Secretary of Defense* (Washington, DC: GPO, 1986), 119-32.

22. For example, the Air Force averaged 3.16 serious mishaps per 100,000 flying hours in 1978. In 1991, the rate was 1.1, the best safety record ever achieved. According to General Powell, the "improvement was largely a result of the increased training that our pilots have received over the past decade, as well as their more modern aircraft, and the increased attention those aircraft receive." *Hearings,Threat Assessment*, 491.

23. *National Journal* 25 (September 18, 1883): 2242.

24. Ibid., 2244.

25. Ibid., 2242.

26. *Hearings, Threat Assessment*, 492.

27. Ibid.

28. Ibid., 492-93.

29. See *Total Force Policy Report to the Congress* (Washington, DC: Department of Defense, 1991).

30. *Structuring U.S. Forces After the Cold War: Costs and Effects of Increased Reliance on the Reserves* (Washington, DC: Congressional Budget Office, 1992), 4-5, 44.

31. Ibid.

32. Ibid, 78.

33. Ibid.

34. Ibid., 27-33.

35. Ibid., 7.

36. Ibid., 9.

37. Ibid., 31.

38. Ibid., 17-18.

39. *Hearings, Threat Assessment,* 492.

40. *U.S. Defense Strategy for a New Era* (Washington, DC: American Security Council Foundation, 1992), 22-23.

41. Ibid., 23.

42. Ibid.

43. *The Economic Effects of Reduced Defense Spending* (Washington, DC: Congressional Budget Office, 1992), 22-23.

44. Ibid., 23.

45. See *U.S. Defense Strategy for a New Era*, 22-29.

46. Ibid., 29-32.

47. *Defense News*, July 12-18, 1993, 1, 12.

48. *Defense News*, July 5-11, 1993, 3.

49. Ibid., 20.

50. Robert Haveman et al., "The European Welfare State in Transition," in *Perspectives on the Reagan Years*, ed. J. L. Palmer (Washington, DC: Urban Institute Press, 1986), 147-73.

51. Ibid., 166.

52. Ibid., 164-66.

53. Ibid., 158.

54. Dennis S. Ippolito, *Uncertain Legacies, Federal Budget Policy from Roosevelt through Reagan* (Charlottesville: University Press of Virginia, 1990), 95.

55. Ibid.

56. *Historical Tables, Budget of the United States Government, Fiscal Year 1990* (Washington, DC: GPO, 1989), 132.

Index

Abrams tank, 158
Acheson, Dean, Secretary
    of State, 12
Afghanistan, Soviet Union
    invasion of, 23
Air Force, budget,
    1955-1960, 13
Apache helicopter, 158
Army, budget, 1955-1960,
    13
Aspen Institute, 59
Aspin, Les, 52
    Humanitarian Aid and
        Stabilization Fund,
        81-83
    Secretary of Defense,
        79, 81-84, 105,
        161-162
    fiscal 1994 budget, 99
    threat-based force
        planning, 85-97
Aspin Plan, 1992, 86t

B-2 bomber program, 158
Baker, James, Secretary of
    State, 82
Balanced Budget and
    Emergency Deficit
    Control
    Reaffirmation Act of
    1987, 42
Base force concept, 84-96
    Bush, 80
    reductions, 94t
Brady, Nicholas F., 72n
British Defense Ministry, 170
Brown, Harold, Secretary of
    Defense, 23
Budget control, comprehensive,
    77-79
Budget Enforcement Act of

1990 (BEA), 39, 50-68, 67t,
    73n
Budget policy context, 1992, 76
Budget process, controls on,
    112-115
Bush, George, 39, 75
Bush administration, 39-45
    1990 budget
        agreement, 49-58
    base force program, 80
    budget policy dilemma,
        143-144
    budget strategy, 60
    budget tradeoffs, 57-58
    budgetary support of
        defense strategy,
        158-159
    defense budget
        cutbacks, 4
    Defense Management
        Review, 61
    discretionary spending, 52,
        76-77
    fiscal year 1990 budget, 40,
        42t, 50
    fiscal year 1991 budget, 44,
        47
    fiscal year 1992 budget, 60,
        62t, 63t, 64t
    fiscal year 1993 budget, 66
    Future Years Defense
        Plan (FYDP), 59
    post-Cold war strategy, 59
    Soviet Union "climate of
        uncertainty," 81
Bush campaign, defense
    strategy, 70

Carter, Jimmy, 22
Carter administration, 22-25
    nonpoor entitlements, 128

177

About the Author

Dennis S. Ippolito is the Eugene McElvaney Professor of Political Science at Southern Methodist University. His books on national political institutions and budget policy include, among others, *Uncertain Legacies, Federal Budget Policy from Roosevelt through Reagan; Hidden Spending: The Politics of Federal Credit Programs*; and *Congressional Spending.*

ISBN 0-16-045229-5